W9-ADD-622

THE CHURCH
AND THE WORKINGMAN

IS VOLUME
104
OF THE

Twentieth Century Encyclopedia of Catholicism

UNDER SECTION
IX
THE CHURCH AND THE MODERN WORLD

IT IS ALSO THE

134TH
VOLUME IN ORDER OF PUBLICATION

THE TWENTIETH CENTURY ENCYCLOPEDIA OF CATHOLICISM

Edited by HENRI DANIEL-ROPS of the Académie Française

THE CHURCH
AND THE WORKINGMAN

By JOHN F. CRONIN, S.S.
and HARRY W. FLANNERY

HAWTHORN BOOKS · PUBLISHERS · *New York*

Copyright © 1965 by Hawthorn Books, Inc., 70 Fifth Avenue, New York City 10011. Copyright under International and Pan-American Copyright Conventions. Philippines Copyright 1965 by Hawthorn Books, Inc. All rights reserved, including the right to reproduce this book, or portions thereof, in any form, except for the inclusion of brief quotations in a review. This book was manufactured in the United States of America and published simultaneously in Canada by Prentice-Hall of Canada, Ltd., 520 Ellesmere Road, Scarborough, Ontario. The Library of Congress has catalogued the Twentieth Century Encyclopedia of Catholicism under card number 58-14327. Library of Congress Catalogue Card Number for this volume: 65-13027.

First Edition, November, 1965

NIHIL OBSTAT

Joseph B. Collins, S.S., S.T.D., Ph.D.

   Censor Deputatus

IMPRIMATUR

✠ Patrick A. O'Boyle

   Archbishop of Washington

Washington, OCTOBER 12, 1965

The nihil obstat and imprimatur are official declarations that a book or pamphlet is free of doctrinal or moral error. No implication is contained therein that those who have granted the nihil obstat and the imprimatur agree with the contents, opinions or statements expressed.

H-9570

CONTENTS

PART I

THE TEACHING OF THE CHURCH
by John F. Cronin, S.S.

PART II

FROM THE INDUSTRIAL REVOLUTION TO THE PRESENT DAY
by Harry W. Flannery

INTRODUCTION

Pope John XXIII said: "It is not enough merely to formulate a social doctrine. It must be translated into reality. And this is particularly true of the Church's social doctrine, the light of which is truth, justice its objective, and love its driving force" (*Mater et Magistra,* 226). These comments afford a fitting introduction to this volume in which the authors present the social teaching of the Catholic Church in the area of labour. At the same time, they indicate how this teaching has been made vital through social action in the world of work. When the so-called labour problem became acute in the nineteenth century, the misery of the workers was a challenge to the consciences of sensitive and sincere men. They sought solutions to the problems of unemployment, the exploitation of the work of women and children, and the frightfully low wages paid in the newly expanding industrial and commercial society. Concrete programmes of action were proposed, such as the organization of workers into unions and the protection of their rights through social legislation. But the reformers also sought principles upon which to base their activities, principles that would confound the two extreme positions of the day, the dominant attitude of *laissez-faire* and the challenging response of socialism. For this reason the Church cannot confine her teaching and her solicitude exclusively to man's spiritual needs. Following the example of her Founder, who not only preached the Gospel, but also multiplied loaves to feed the hungry, she seeks to present a total view of life and a complete philosophy of life. Part of this philosophy, both as theory and as social action, will appear in these pages.

SOURCES

Except for the teachings of Pius XII, most of the citations in the pages to follow come from five outstanding social encyclicals. These are listed below in chronological order and reference will normally be made to the Latin or English title of these documents. In the case of Pius XII, the customary reference will be the date of the document or message, unless its title is widely known. In general, the translation used for Pope Pius XII is taken from *The Pope Speaks,* a valuable quarterly that republishes papal documents. Occasionally, the text is taken from the National Catholic Welfare Conference (NCWC) News Service.

Rerum Novarum, "On the Condition of Workers," 1891 encyclical of Leo XIII. The NCWC edition is used.

Quadragesimo Anno, "On Reconstructing the Social Order," 1931 encyclical of Pius XI. The NCWC edition is used.

On Atheistic Communism, 1937 encyclical of Pope Pius XI. The NCWC edition is used.

Mater et Magistra, "Christianity and Social Progress," 1961 encyclical of Pope John XXIII. *The Pope Speaks* edition is used.

Pacem in Terris, "Peace on Earth," 1963 encyclical of Pope John XXIII. *The Pope Speaks* edition is used.

John F. Cronin, S.S.,
Harry W. Flannery,
Washington, D.C.
August, 1965

PART I

THE TEACHING OF THE CHURCH

By

JOHN F. CRONIN, S.S.

CHAPTER I

MAN AND SOCIETY

Fundamental to the social teaching of the Catholic Church is her position on the dignity of man and the function of society. Man's dignity springs from his nature as a child of God, created with an immortal soul. Because man has reason and free will he is a subject of both rights and duties. He knows that the spark of the immortal infused in him by the Almighty raises him to a higher and nobler level than any other form of life on this earth. He is, under God, lord and master of the universe. All things exist to serve him, as he exists to serve God.

Christian doctrine goes beyond this natural-law concept of human dignity. The Christian is spoken of as the adopted son of God, the temple of the Holy Spirit, an adopted brother of Christ. He shares through grace the very life of God in a mysterious manner, and he is called to eternal union with God in heaven. Consequently, "no one may with impunity outrage the dignity of man, which God himself treats with great reverence, nor impede his course to that level of perfection which accords with eternal life in heaven" (*Rerum Novarum*, 57).

THE RIGHTS OF MAN

From this dignity flow the basic rights of man. First of these is the right to life itself. One must respect the life and the integrity of another. It is wrong to kill, to maim, or in any serious way to diminish the life of another person, except

for compelling reasons such as self-defence. The sacredness
of human life has been acknowledged throughout history.

Living is not mere survival. Man's right to live means that
he should be able to live as befits a human being. He
should be allowed to marry and to rear children properly.
From this it follows that he should be able to give to his
family a suitable home, adequate food and clothing, an education fitted to their needs, considering the state of the culture of his time and place, proper medical care and some
security for the future.

In our day, the normal way to achieve economic security
is through work. A man may till the soil, mine the earth,
work in a factory, or operate an electronic calculator. He
may work for himself, with his own tools and property, or
he may work for another. If he works for another, he may be
paid an hourly wage or a salary. It is possible that his wife
and children may also work. But if this work means the
absence from the home of a mother of young children, then
family life may suffer. When young children work in a fashion that is detrimental to their health or their education, their
lives have been injured and diminished.

Thus we begin to see how one basic right leads to another.
The right to live may well imply the right to a job. It will
affect the morality of wages and the propriety of employing
mothers of young children. Labour relations also involve the
human dignity of the worker. "Workers are not to be treated
as slaves; justice demands that the dignity of the human personality be respected in them, ennobled as it has been
through what we call the Christian character" (*Rerum Novarum,* 31).

Pius XII asks that the type of work be such as to command the active and intelligent interest of the worker, if this
be at all possible. "The worker then feels that he is using not
only his muscular power but also his very soul, and that his
labour is recompensed, first of all, by pride in the work ac-
complished, which grows in him. Instead of seeing in his work
only a means for making a living, he finds in it a sense of life

and the measure of his personal and social being" (January 10th, 1958). John XXIII is even stronger in his expression of this thought. "If the whole structure and organization of an economic system is such as to compromise human dignity, to lessen a man's sense of responsibility or rob him of the opportunity for exercising personal initiative, then such a system, we maintain, is altogether unjust—no matter how much wealth it produces, or how justly and equitably such wealth is distributed" (*Mater et Magistra,* 83).

It is clear, then, that such phrases as the dignity of man and the rights of man are more than poetic expressions. They have profound implications for economic and political life, as will be more evident in the pages to follow. Many of the tragic abuses in modern society stem from a faulty concept of man's dignity and rights, or from an unwillingness to recognize these rights. For example, the ugly stain of racism which preoccupies Americans and others these days involves a denial of the equal dignity of all men. While men differ in talent, education, culture, character, personality, and numerous other traits, they enjoy a basic equality before God because of the dignity of their nature. They should enjoy a similar equality before the law. "The Church does not promise that absolute equality which others are proclaiming because she knows that life in human society always and of necessity produces a whole range of degrees and differences in physical and mental traits, in inward dispositions and inclinations, in occupations and in responsibilities. But at the same time, she assures you of full equality in human dignity . . ." (Pius XII, October 31st, 1948).

Although men are equal in their right to access to the fruits of the earth for their livelihood, the Church recognizes that there must be reasonable processes for the exploitation of nature's abundant riches. Thus mankind has generally held that private ownership of property is necessary for the orderly, peaceful, and efficient use of material goods. The Church has sanctioned this right against socialists and communists, who call for varied degrees of common ownership. "The right of private ownership of goods, including productive goods, has permanent validity. It is part of the natural order, which teaches that the individual is prior to society and that society must be ordered to the good of the individual" (*Mater et Magistra,* 109).

This defence of private property is by no means an endorsement of gross inequalities in the distribution of income and wealth. "The Church defends the right of private property, a right she considers fundamentally inalienable. But she insists also on the need for a more just distribution of property and deplores the unnatural social situation in which an enormous mass of impoverished people live beside a small group of the very rich and privileged" (Pius XII, March 11th, 1951).

MAN IN SOCIETY

While the discussion thus far has centred upon the individual and his rights, there have been frequent references to economic and political society. This is as it should be. Man is not merely an individual; he lives in society. I have already alluded to the most fundamental of human societies, the family. The family is a basic element in any social structure. "Religion and the reality of the past teach that the social structures, such as matrimony and family, the community and professional groups, social union in personal property, are essential cells which secure man's freedom and, along with it, his function in history" (Pius XII, Christmas, 1956).

One of the highest forms of society is the civil State:

God has likewise destined man for civil society according to the dictates of his very nature. In the plan of the Creator, society is a natural means which man can and must use to reach his destined end. Society is for man and not *vice versa.* . . . It is society which affords the opportunities for the development of all the individual and social gifts bestowed on human nature. . . . Only man, the human person, and not society in any form is endowed with reason and a morally free will (*On Atheistic Communism,* 29).

When we say that man is social by nature, we mean that his physical, mental, and emotional life demands the company of others. The child requires a mother and father for survival and sustenance. But even for adult life, there is need for organization and specialization, if this planet is to support the millions of human beings who inhabit it. The solitary hunter or trapper is the exception among mankind.

Our mental development depends upon the teaching of others. This can mean formal schooling, or the reading of books, or even the intelligent observation of the conduct of other persons. In the give and take of social living, our minds, wills, and characters grow and become strong. The family that overprotects and overshelters a child cripples it psychologically and emotionally.

The emotional side of our nature likewise drives us to seek the company of others. The desire to love and be loved is quite basic in mankind. Moreover, we cherish friendship, companionship, and membership in various societies. Indeed, the right to associate is considered fundamental. One of the greatest tyrannies of the totalitarian State is its monopoly control over man's social life. Life is deeply impoverished when the State and its approved organizations are the only outlet for man's social needs.

It should be clear from all that has been said that society is a much broader concept than civil government. The State is but one of the many societies which men by nature tend to form. There are also religious, economic, professional, cultural, and recreational groups. The social club, the labour union, and the trade association are normal human developments. So are bridge clubs and leagues for the promotion of square dancing. We even have large assemblies gathered for the purpose of improving the breed of horses.

The relationship between the individual and society is not

easily explained. Pius XI was quoted above as saying "Society is for man and not *vice versa*". This statement is true, but it can easily be misunderstood. While society exists to help man, man in turn needs society and cannot normally thrive without it. Man makes the rules for society, but social living in turn demands rules and laws and obedience to such regulations.

Recent popes have devoted a major portion of their social teachings to the proper relationship between man and society. In the time of Leo XIII and even Pius XI, there was a strong need to assert the rights and prerogatives of society against a dominant individualism. Individualism is a self-centred philosophy which exalts only the rights of the individual, but minimizes or denies his duties towards others. It can lead to the jungle law of the survival of the fittest. In economic life it led to exploitation of workers, waste of natural resources, and a shameless, materialistic greed. In more recent times we have heard much of group individualism, in which organized pressure groups seek only the selfish concerns of their members, even to the detriment of the general welfare.

At the other extreme, and this was the particular burden of Pius XII, there was the tendency towards excessive social concentration of power. This pope was deeply worried over centralized power which threatened individual liberty, whether such power was exercised by economic monopolies, by labour unions, or by totalitarian States. It is obvious that he shared the fear that power corrupts, and absolute power corrupts absolutely. Still more recently, in the pontificate of John XXIII, there was another concern over the relationships between society and the individual. Pope John wrote of socialization, "an increase in social relationships, in those mutual ties, that is, which grow daily more numerous and which have led to the introduction of many and varied forms of associations in the lives and activities of citizens, and their acceptance within our legal framework" (*Mater et Magistra,* 59).

This trend expresses itself in the growing intervention of the State in the lives of individuals. But it also results from man's natural inclination to join, and has given rise to "both national and international movements, associations, and institutions with economic, cultural, social, sporting, recreational, professional, and political ends" (*Mater et Magistra,* 60). Pope John could see many advantages from the more highly organized social life of our times. It leads to higher living standards and more leisure and recreation. It can enlarge our field of knowledge through modern methods of travel and communication, such as radio, television, the cinema, and jet aircraft. But it can also be a restrictive influence upon individuals, a source of pressure towards conformity, thus making it "difficult for a person to think independently of outside influences, to act upon his own initiative, exercise his responsibility, and express and fulfil his own personality" (*Mater et Magistra,* 62).

While John XXIII does not speak of Madison Avenue, the organization man, subliminal advertising, or Riesman's other-directed society, it is obvious that he is aware of these trends in modern life. Yet he is not dismayed at what he sees. He takes the view that what man creates, man can control and make subject to the moral law and a sound concept of society. We are not being relentlessly forced into the status of robots by our computerized age. We can still determine the tone and direction of society, and it is our duty to be its master, not its servant.

One principle that is helpful in regulating social life is called the principle of subsidiarity. Speaking of the civil State, John XXIII says:

> In this work of directing, stimulating, supplying, and integrating, its guiding principle must be the "principle of subsidiary function" formulated by Pius XI in *Quadragesimo Anno.* "This is a fundamental principle of social philosophy, unshaken and unchangeable. . . . Just as it is wrong to withdraw from the individual and commit to a community what private enterprise and industry can accomplish, so too it is an injustice, a grave evil, and a disturbance of the right order,

for a larger and higher association to arrogate to itself functions which can be performed efficiently by smaller and lower
societies. Of its very nature the true aim of all social activity
should be to help members of the social body, but never to
destroy or absorb them" (*Mater et Magistra,* 53).

There are two aspects to the principle just quoted. One
is negative in nature, namely, the prohibition directed towards larger and more powerful groups, forbidding them to
take over the functions of smaller and weaker bodies. The
other, and more positive, aspect can be derived from the
very title of the principle. It is the duty of society to "subsi-
dize" the individual in the original sense of the term—
subsidy meaning aid, support, assistance. Social life gives
the individual the opportunity to do many things that he
could not do by himself alone.

A MORAL SOCIETY

Now we have the basic principles from which we can
construct a picture of man and society. We base this picture
on the nature of man as an individual and as a member of
society. Our interpretation follows the moral guidance of the
Church, to which is committed the task of explaining the
entirety of God's law, which means both natural law as
learned by reason as we study God's purpose in creating
man, and the divine positive law as learned through reve-
lation. We begin with the dignity of man and his basic
rights, including the right to live and the derivative rights
to a decent job, to a wage sufficient for himself and his family, and to the recognition of his dignity in the conditions
that surround his work. We note that this right is exercised
in society, first of all in economic society. Economic society in turn has taken various forms throughout history and
in different nations of the world.

Yet, as a general rule in the complex world of today, one
of the prime characteristics of economic life is the scope
given to individual initiative. "It should be stated at the

outset that in the economic order first place must be given to the personal initiative of private citizens working either as individuals or in association with each other in various ways for the furtherance of common interests" (*Mater et Magistra,* 51). This principle should be self-evident, since the purpose of any society is to help the individual, not to absorb him or deny his rights. Closely connected with this concept of private initiative is the institution of private property. Private ownership leads to order, peace, and efficiency in the utilization of the earth's bounty. This, of course, is a general rule which does not preclude public ownership when this is genuinely demanded by the general welfare. "For certain kinds of property, it is rightly contended, ought to be reserved to the State, since they carry with them a dominating power so great that they cannot without danger to the general welfare be entrusted to private individuals" (*Quadragesimo Anno,* 114).

But private initiative and ownership do not imply the absolute right to do what one pleases with a property or business. This is so because the exercise of the rights of one individual affects the rights of others. Thus the conduct of a business by its owner must take into account the welfare of workers and the legitimate interests of consumers.

> First, then, let it be considered as certain and established that neither Leo nor those theologians who have taught under the guidance and authority of the Church have ever denied or questioned the twofold character of ownership, usually called individual and social according as it regards either separate persons or the common good. For they have always unanimously maintained that nature, rather the Creator himself, has given man the right of private ownership, not only that individuals may be able to provide for themselves and their families, but also that the goods which the Creator destined for the entire family of mankind may through this institution truly serve this purpose. All this can be achieved in nowise except through the maintenance of a certain and definite order (*Quadragesimo Anno,* 45).

> It follows from what We have termed the individual and at the same time social character of ownership, that men

must consider in this matter not only their own advantage but also the common good. To define these duties in detail when necessity requires and natural law has not done so, is the function of those in charge of the state. Therefore, public authority, under the guiding light always of the natural and divine law, can determine more accurately upon consideration of the true requirements of the common good, what is permitted and what is not permitted to owners in the use of their property. (*Quadragesimo Anno,* 49).

John XXIII states the same principle in the paragraph immediately following his defence of private initiative. "But —for reasons explained by our predecessors—the civil power must also have a hand in the economy. It has to promote production in a way best calculated to achieve social progress and the well-being of citizens" (*Mater et Magistra,* 52).

Accordingly, while we extol private initiative and property as fundamental in our economic system, there must be concern for the rights of others and the common good of society. Property owners have obligations as well as rights. These rules can be spelled out by the State, when the common good demands. But this requirement should be understood in terms of the principle of subsidiarity, explained earlier. When possible, social controls should be exercised by intermediate bodies, such as labour unions or trade associations, for example.

This concept of intermediate bodies is a special contribution of Pius XI, although other popes have expressed similar principles. This pope called for a radical reconstruction of social order. Such reforms meant, not merely the willingness of men of good will to follow justice and charity, but also the embodiment of these principles in the laws, customs, and institutions of society. Good will alone is not enough, since there are bound to be persons of lower ideals who will strive to impair the moral climate of a country. There must be some legislative sanction to ensure that proper standards are widely observed in the economic community.

Yet it would be wrong to assume that the establishment of

proper codes in the world of business, industry, and finance should be the exclusive function of civil government. If our only recourse in the face of an abuse is to legislation, then the State will be overburdened by excessive cares and duties. It is much better to introduce a broad pattern of self-regulation by economic groups which can act as buffers between the individual and the firm, on the one hand, and the civil State on the other. Needless to say, this principle applies to areas other than economic life, but our concern at the moment is with the world of labour.

Methods for working out such an infrastructure will vary according to the culture, customs, and laws of a given people. The actual illustrations used in *Quadragesimo Anno* were expressed against a background of Roman law. They envisaged organizations in which membership would be compulsory and whose regulations would be binding on members. To use an arbitrary example, in the automotive industry both labour and management would be represented on joint boards empowered to set basic standards for the industry. Such boards might set up codes of fair competition, basic protections for the rights of workers, and possibly uniform social-security benefits, such as pensions and health plans. This process would not replace collective bargaining in which the parties would urge their separate, rather than their common, interests.

It may well be that this Roman-law approach would be psychologically and even legally deficient in nations whose legal systems are based on English common law. We may be inclined to use somewhat different methods to secure the same results. For example, industry-wide collective bargaining may set up common patterns which embody justice and equity in the labour-relations systems of the member firms. Thus we accept the basic social principles laid down by Pius XI, but implement them according to our own customs and genius. Undoubtedly this difference of approach led John XXIII, in *Mater et Magistra,* to emphasize the fundamental ideals of his predecessor rather than the Roman-law elaboration of these principles.

Because the Church issues warnings against excessive concentration of power in the State, it does not follow that she opposes social legislation as a major part of the solution of the so-called labour question. This point will be elaborated subsequently in Chapter VI. It is obvious from a reading of the great papal social documents that the Holy See is constantly engaged in balancing trends and principles. In the nineteenth century, when social legislation was often of minor import, Pope Leo XIII could call for laws to protect the rights of workers. After World War II, when some nations embarked on extensive programmes of nationalization of industry, Pius XII would caution against excessive concentration of power in the State.

Always we must distinguish between goals and techniques for achieving these goals. Our basic aim is a society which respects and fosters the rights and the dignity of the individual and the family. At one moment in history, these rights may be threatened by the exploitation of workers by industry. At another period, the individual may find government seriously encroaching on his rights. Even the same methods may produce different results in various parts of the world. Thus union pressures for equality with management resulted in codetermination laws in Germany. By contrast, in the United States, similar pressures were largely directed at changing working conditions through collective bargaining.

In the pages to follow, the authors will try to make clear a distinction between social principles of the Church, and the concrete application of these principles at a given time and place. Sometimes there is a wide area of agreement among Catholic social scientists and theologians on the interpretation and application of principles. At other times there may be sharp differences of opinion, based largely upon a different assessment of the concrete economic and social environment.

John XXIII gives some wise observations on this situation.

> Differences of opinion in the application of principles can sometimes arise even among sincere Catholics. When this happens, they should be careful not to lose their respect and esteem for each other. Instead, they should strive to find points of agreement for effective and suitable action, and not wear themselves out in interminable arguments and, under the pretext of the better or the best, omit to do the good that is possible and therefore obligatory (*Mater et Magistra,* 238).

One can hardly overstress the wisdom of John XXIII's comment on the "good that is possible and therefore obligatory". The social teaching of the Church is not an ivory-tower system designed to please the academic world. It is a code of conduct and a call to action.

CHAPTER II

A LIVING WAGE

The concept of a living wage is at the same time one of the great contributions of the Church to social theory and a perfect example of the areas of dispute among Catholics to which John XXIII referred. As the historical sections of this volume indicate, labour was severely exploited in the nineteenth century. While this exploitation was deplored by men of good will everywhere, there was no wide agreement on the moral principles governing wages.

Employers generally defended their position by legal and economic arguments. Their legal position was that the wage involved a contract between worker and employer. Since this contract was freely entered upon, it was legally binding. Moreover, the economic theory widely prevalent at the time held that any tampering with free competition would lead to an extensive waste of resources. A worker whose wage represented less than the value of his contribution to a firm could seek work elsewhere. A competing employer would recognize his worth. By contrast, if the worker was paid more than the value of his contribution, the employer would find that his costs were too high for effective competition in the market.

Many economists held that the Iron Law of Wages of necessity forced workers to remain at poverty levels. According to this view, the fund available for wages was limited. But the pressure of population growth was unlimited. Hence, according to the law of supply and demand, there would always tend to be more workers than available jobs.

Competition for such jobs would drive wages down to the subsistence level. Sickness and even starvation would then achieve a balance between workers and jobs at this minimum level.

Revolting as were such doctrines, they were widely held in the industrial world of the nineteenth century. Even theologians who deplored the results of these theories did not feel free to combat the reasoning behind them. In particular, they often held that justice demanded that a wage contract be enforced. Hence the only solution for the wretched condition of workers was to be found in works of charity. Not all Catholics agreed with this position, as is clearly shown elsewhere in this book. Finally, Leo XIII spoke out.

A MORAL WAGE

Leo XIII did not accept the notion of a limited wage fund available for the needs of workers. On the contrary, they have every right to share equitably in the wealth that they help produce.

> It is incontestable that the wealth of nations arises from no other source than the labour of workers. Equity therefore commands that public authority show proper concern for the worker so that from what he contributes to the common good he may receive what will enable him, housed, clothed, and secure, to live his life without hardship. Whence it follows that all those measures ought to be favoured which seem in any way capable of benefiting the condition of workers. Such solicitude is so far from injuring anyone, that it is destined rather to benefit all, because it is of absolute interest to the State that those citizens should not be miserable in every respect from whom such necessary goods proceed (*Rerum Novarum,* 51).

Here Leo XIII lays down the principle that a proper share of the wealth of nations must go to the workers whose labour produces this wealth. He does not, of course, accept the Marxist concept that labour is the sole source of production. This is evident elsewhere in the Encyclical when he rejects

socialism. But certainly labour is entitled to a proportionate
share of the national wealth, a share that permits workers to
live as befits human beings.

This reasoning must affect our concept of a proper wage.
Leo XIII analyses the accepted theory that "free consent
fixes the amount of the wage". He argues that this theory
looks at only one element in the wage contract, namely, the
personal choice of the worker. But work is something more
than a matter of personal choice. It is also necessary to sustain life. "Hence arises necessarily the right of securing things
to sustain life, and only a wage earned by his labour gives a
poor man the means to acquire these things" (*Rerum
Novarum,* 62).

One could supplement Leo XIII's argument here by ques-
tioning the alleged freedom of contract involved in the wage
agreement. When a worker was confronted with the choice
of accepting a given wage, or condemning himself and his
family to misery and starvation, there was no real freedom
of choice. Moreover, the average worker did not have access
to the information needed to bargain effectively with an employer, even if individual bargaining would be in fact useful.
About the only real recourse of needy workers was the hope
that in other lands, such as America or Australia, they could
find more opportunity. Actually, Leo XIII did not use this
argument explicitly. Rather he noted that

> there is always underlying such agreements an element of
> natural justice, and one greater and more ancient than the
> free consent of contracting parties, namely, that the wage
> shall not be less than enough to support a worker who is
> thrifty and upright. If compelled by necessity or moved by
> fear of a worse evil, a worker accepts a harder condition,
> which although against his will he must accept because the
> employer or contractor imposes it, he certainly submits to
> force, against which justice cries out in protest (*Rerum
> Novarum,* 63).

Certainly by implication these final observations question the
validity of an exploitive wage contract, even though Leo
XIII did not explicitly face this point.

Thus was posed a momentous papal challenge to the existing wage theories of the nineteenth century. Nor was the Encyclical content to lay down this principle, without suggesting means for implementing it. Later the right of workers to join together in unions was endorsed. Likewise the duty of the State to protect the rights of the poor and the oppressed was asserted. But papal doctrine on a living wage raised questions as it was answering others. Theologians in particular disputed as to the scope of a living wage. Is this to be a wage sufficient to support an individual worker in decent comfort, or must it as well be adequate to meet the needs of his family? In the United States of America, a young theologian faced this challenge as he wrote his doctoral dissertation on the living wage. This priest, Fr John A. Ryan, argued that justice demanded a family wage. He further insisted that this wage was the first claim on the returns of a firm, prior to profits, interest on investment, and rent on land.

Pius XI endorsed the family-wage position taken by Fr Ryan. "Every effort must therefore be made that fathers of families receive a wage large enough to meet ordinary family needs adequately" (*Quadragesimo Anno,* 71). Again he states:

> Social justice cannot be said to have been satisfied as long as working men are denied a salary that will enable them to secure proper sustenance for themselves and their families; as long as they are denied the opportunity of acquiring a modest fortune and forestalling the plague of universal pauperism; as long as they cannot make suitable provision through public or private insurance for old age, for periods of illness or unemployment (*On Atheistic Communism,* 52).

Still elsewhere he demands that "in the state such economic and social methods should be adopted as will enable every head of a family to earn as much as, according to his station in life, is necessary for himself, his wife, and for the rearing of his children . . ." (*Casti Connubii*).

Does this mean that every employer has a moral obligation to pay a family wage, regardless of business conditions and the economic value of a worker's contribution? This point will be examined more at length later in this chapter, but it is pertinent here to note some relevant comments of Pius XI on the problem of employers' obligations.

He notes, for example, that work has social as well as individual aspects. Workers cannot produce properly unless society is properly organized. "Therefore, where the social and individual nature of work is neglected, it will be impossible to evaluate work justly and pay it according to justice" (*Quadragesimo Anno,* 69). This point was overlooked by many theologians, who held that employers must pay a living wage regardless of general economic and social conditions.

Pius XI himself was much more cautious in imposing obligations on individual employers caught in an unjust economic situation. Thus he held that the condition of the business must be taken into account, "for it would be unjust to demand excessive wages which a business cannot stand without its ruin and consequent calamity to the workers" (*Quadragesimo Anno,* 72). This would not be the case if low wages resulted from inefficiency on the part of management. But if the source of inadequate pay is unfair competition, then those who bring about such conditions "are guilty of grave wrong".

Employers and workers alike must "strive with united strength" to overcome these difficulties and obstacles and public authorities should assist them in this effort. "If, however, matters come to an extreme crisis, it must finally be considered whether the business can continue or the workers are to be cared for in some other way" (*Quadragesimo Anno,* 73).

Again Pius XI shows moderation when he observes that it

happens all too frequently, however, under the salary system that individual employers are helpless to insure justice unless, with a view to its practice, they organize institutions the object of which is to prevent competition incompatible with fair treatment for the workers. Where this is true, it is the duty of contractors and employers to support and promote such necessary organizations as normal instruments enabling them to fulfil their obligations of justice (*On Atheistic Communism,* 53).

These points should be studied carefully, lest we fall into the snare of imposing heavy burdens on men, without lifting a finger to help them. The primary obligation of the employer is to cooperate in such social and economic reforms as enable a worker to earn a living wage.

JOHN XXIII ON WAGE JUSTICE

John XXIII also asserted that the determination of wages should not be left to the laws of the market place. "It must be determined in accordance with justice and equity; which means that workers must be paid a wage which allows them to live a truly human life and to fulfil their family obligations in a worthy manner" (*Mater et Magistra,* 71). But he also noted that other factors must be considered in determining wage justice. These include: "the effective contribution which each individual makes to the economic effort, the financial state of the company for which he works, the requirements of the general good of the particular country— having regard particularly to the repercussions on the overall employment of the working force in the country as a whole— and finally the requirements of the common good of the universal family of nations of every kind, both large and small" (*Ibid.*).

He held that these principles have universal validity. "But the degree of their applicability to concrete cases cannot be determined without reference to the quantity and quality of available resources; and these can—and in fact do—vary from country to country, and even, from time to time, within the same country" (*Mater et Magistra,* 72).

Although the language is different, there is no substantial variation in the wage teaching of John XXIII from that of his predecessors. He also asserts that there is a moral obligation to pay a living wage, but that its implementation depends on certain economic factors. Wages should be determined in part by the condition of a firm and the worker's contribution, but they are also affected by considerations of the general common good and the resources available at a given time and place.

Pope John was particularly careful to spell out the demands of the common good.

> On the national level they include: employment of the greatest possible number of workers; care lest privileged classes arise, even among the workers; maintenance of an equilibrium between wages and prices; the need to make goods and services accessible to the greatest number; elimination, or at least the restriction, of inequalities in the various branches of the economy—that is, between agriculture, industry, and services; creation of a proper balance between economic expansion and the development of social services, especially through the activity of public authorities; the best possible adjustment of the means of production to the progress of science and technology; seeing to it that the benefits which make possible a more human way of life will be available not merely to the present generation but to the coming generations as well (*Mater et Magistra*, 79).

This extensive list of requirements could well be considered the spelling out in detail of the social and individual character of work, as mentioned by Pius XI. Wage policy should be one of the factors in securing a general economic balance in a nation. Thus we should not have a privileged class of very highly paid workers, while others are poorly paid. Wages should not rise to the point of causing unemployment. They should be roughly equal in the major segments of the economy, agriculture, industry, and service occupations. Wage increases should not normally cause price increases, much less lead to inflation. In this way economic expansion will lead to social progress.

There is also the international common good to be considered. This involves: "the avoidance of all forms of unfair competition between the economies of different countries;

the fostering of mutual collaboration and good will; and effective co-operation in the development of economically less
advanced countries" (*Mater et Magistra,* 80).

Economists probably would agree that most of these requirements would be more readily met if the fruits of ad-
vancing productivity were reflected more in lower prices
than in higher wages. In the United States, for example, the
most productive sectors are agriculture and industry. Farm
prices of agricultural products are quite low, even after artifi-
cial governmental attempts to secure higher prices. Yet factory prices of industrial products are not lowered, despite the
enormous gains in efficiency resulting from modernization
and automation. Consequently farmers and farm workers do
not share in the growth of the national economy. Likewise
public servants and those in service occupations tend to fall
behind. In the international sphere, many nations, especially
developing nations, find extreme difficulty in buying the products of American industry.

Without elaborating further at this time on papal notions
of wage justice, it is clear that this doctrine is fairly complex
and sophisticated. It is not a simple matter of a worker tell-
ing an employer that the latter has a moral obligation to pay
him a wage adequate for family needs. Nor is it quite as
simple as it appeared to Fr Ryan in 1906, when he claimed
that such a wage had moral priority over profits, interest,
and rent.

THE MEANING OF A LIVING WAGE

We are now in a position to gather together the strands
of papal teaching and to attempt to spell out the precise
meaning of the living wage. It is clear that the worker is entitled in justice to a wage adequate to support him and his
family in decent conditions. In effect, this means an income
sufficient to allow him to buy or rent a good home. The
family should be able to afford wholesome and nutritious

food. It should have access to suitable education and adequate medical care. There should be provision for unemployment, old age, and exceptionally onerous family burdens.

The securing of such a wage, or non-wage income if needed, is not primarily a matter of negotiations between the worker and his employer, although we shall note later that collective bargaining does have a part to play. The employer does have an obligation in strict justice to pay the worker an amount equal to the value contributed by the worker's services. In practice, it is rarely possible for a firm to determine accurately what is this contribution, unless in some cases a fair piecework system of payment can be devised. Usually the so-called going wage, determined by law, collective bargaining, or by the labour market, may be considered the strict moral obligation of an employer.

If matters rested here, there would be little improvement over conditions that appalled Leo XIII, at least for those workers whose wages are dependent on the law of supply and demand in the marketplace. But an employer's obligation does not stop with the payment of the minimum due in strict justice. He is also obliged, together with other members of society, to seek reforms that enhance the productivity of labour and hence make possible the payment of a higher wage. We shall note later the economic and political implications of this statement.

For the moment, we need to face up to another moral problem. If a worker has a right to a family wage, what is to be said about the fact that family obligations differ greatly in any given work force? A plant may have a number of unmarried workers; others may be married, but with working wives and no children; still others may be supporting wives and numerous offspring. Assuming equal pay for equal work, both as a matter of justice and a practical necessity in a single plant, whose needs should determine what is a family living wage? If we pick the so-called average family in stating the requirements of wage justice, then there will be a bonus for unmarried workers or those with working wives. Yet the needs of men with larger than average families will not be met.

Common sense here indicates that the wage should involve, as far as possible, a fair distribution of the returns received by the individual company. Moreover, we should seek needed economic adjustments so that this company in turn will be receiving a proper share of the national income. We would hope that every employer would be able to pay a basic wage that is an equitable reflection of the economic resources and productive capacity of the nation.

Supplementing this wage would be various social services geared more to the uneven needs of individuals and families. For example, in countries that do not have national health-service plans, employers may offer medical benefits to workers and their families. Retirement and pension plans, whether governmental or private, can be tailored to family needs. Thus widows with dependent children would receive higher benefits than widows without such obligations, even though their late husbands paid identical amounts into the system.

A policy of taxation that gives allowances for dependents and also for medical expenses over a certain minimum gives some relief to families that have unusual obligations. Many countries go beyond this and have family-allowance systems, either on a governmental or an industry basis. Free public education and easily available scholarships and loans for higher education can also help equalize opportunities for all families.

Devices such as these were clearly meant in John XXIII's numerous references to the need for social progress to keep pace with economic progress, and in his insistence that taxation can be used to bring about a fairer distribution of wealth and income. In wealthy industrial countries, there is no excuse for substantial pockets of deep poverty. There should be combined action by private and public bodies to ensure employment for those who are able and willing to work. Economic adjustments should be made so that this work will

enable a worker to earn at least a basic wage suitable for
family needs. For those who cannot work, there should be
economic aid given in an atmosphere of dignity and com-
passion. Nothing less will satisfy the demands of justice and
equity. Nothing less is acceptable in terms of human dignity.

THE ECONOMICS OF A LIVING WAGE

Social encyclicals understandably do not spell out, except
in most general terms, the economics of a living wage. This
is a technical matter for political leaders, economists, industrialists, engineers, and labour officials. Its technical aspects lie
outside the competence of moralists. When Pius XI noted
unfair competition as a factor in bringing wages down to
the subsistence level, he did indicate one area where improvement might be possible. If all employers in a given industry adopt comparable wage rates and employment conditions, this will largely remove the element of wages from
competition in that industry. Such uniformity is largely
achieved by collective bargaining with unions, although
minimum-wage laws can help in non-union industries that
pay low wages. Historically, such pressures have been the
major factor in raising living standards in industrial nations
throughout the world.

There are limitations in this approach taken by itself. It
may bring about a fairer distribution of national income, but
it does not directly increase that income. If employers have
been reaping exorbitant profits, redistribution of income
can be substantially helpful. But many industries that pay
low wages often afford the owners little or no profits. Under
these circumstances wage increases may lead to price increases. These in turn might cause a decline in the demand
for the products or services involved and consequent unemployment. This is not always a reason to refrain from asking
higher wages under these circumstances, but it is a factor
that must be seriously considered.

Wage pressures can, however, lead to a higher national

product in many cases. They do this by stimulating employers to higher efficiency. For example, higher labour costs may make it profitable to introduce labour-saving machinery. While this is designed to displace workers, it enhances the per-person output of those who remain. Even allowing for depreciation costs on the new machinery, the total value of output has increased sufficiently to justify higher wages without price increases.

There are other ways for increasing efficiency and thus making higher wages economically feasible. Incentive and profit-sharing systems may tap unused resources in the work force itself. Managements faced with the need for cutting costs may study their production methods and increase efficiency even without the introduction of new machinery. Firms may set aside funds for research to develop new and better products. They may cut overheads by seeking broader markets through advertising, aggressive salesmanship, and even the development of overseas subsidiaries.

Nineteenth-century economists with their concepts of a fixed wage fund, and their Marxist followers with their fixation on exploitation of workers, failed to realize that workers are the prime consumers of the output of industry and agriculture. As living standards rise by methods such as those described above, industry finds that it has broad untapped internal markets. When output rises, many firms will find unit costs declining and hence are in a position to pay still higher wages.

The relatively high living standards in the Scandinavian countries, in Canada, in the United States of America, and in the Federal Republic of Germany testify to the workings of the process just noted. This is undoubtedly one of the factors that make the development of the Common Market in Europe one of the most promising economic and political developments in the twentieth century.

In the developing nations of the world, especially in Africa, Asia, and Latin America, there is awareness of the tremendous possibilities open to them. They are no longer

content to remain in the poverty, ignorance, and misery
that has been their lot for centuries. Modern methods of
communication have left them aware of the benefits that
have accrued to workers in other lands. They too want
their share of the earth's bounties. Their special problems
will be treated more at length in Chapter V, but it is pertinent here to note that John XXIII formulated a wage doctrine in such broad terms that it applies to the needs of developing nations as well as to conditions in industrial countries.

Moreover, even with the rapid changes that have taken
place throughout the world since World War II, we are only
at the beginning of the technological revolution of our times.

Surely a world that has shown such versatility in the physical aspects of production should be able to distribute this
abundance in such a fashion as to make poverty and need
mere footnotes in the pages of history. To some this may
seem to be an exciting dream. But to the popes of the social
encyclicals it is a challenge to promote the physical welfare
of every man.

CHAPTER III

THE CHURCH
AND UNIONS

In connection with the living wage, reference was made to the rôle of trade unions and collective bargaining in securing the rights of workers. Collective bargaining is based on a very simple principle, namely, that workers acting in concert are much stronger economically and politically than the same persons functioning as isolated individuals. Organized labour is normally in a position to hire lawyers, accountants, economists, and other specialists who can assist in collective bargaining. If an impasse is reached, the union can withhold the labour of the work force and usually bring about a stoppage of production. While the lack of wages during a strike is a hardship to workers, the employer is also under severe economic pressure to secure a settlement.

By contrast, the individual worker is rarely informed when bargaining with an employer about wages, hours, and working conditions. Even if he were able to present his case skilfully, he usually has little bargaining power should disagreements arise. Except in rare cases, he needs the job far more than the job needs him. His normal recourse is either to accept the terms offered or seek work elsewhere. This latter alternative is rarely appealing to a person with family responsibilities, especially if a large number of unemployed workers are competing for jobs.

It was this logic that drove exploited workers, particularly during the nineteenth and early twentieth centuries, to join labour unions. But this was not always feasible. As John XXIII noted, "the status of trade unions varied in different countries. They were either forbidden, tolerated or recognized as having private legal personality only" (*Mater et Magistra,* 11). In many countries, bitter and even bloody struggles marked the rise of organized labour.

THE RIGHT TO ORGANIZE

It was against this background that Leo XIII asserted the moral right of workers to organize.

> Pope Leo XIII also defended the worker's natural right to enter into association with his fellows. Such associations may consist either of workers alone or of workers and employers, and should be structured in a way best calculated to safeguard the workers' legitimate professional interests. And it is the natural right of the workers to work without hindrance, freely, and on their own initiative within these associations for the achievement of these ends (*Mater et Magistra,* 22).

Leo XIII argued that it is "a right of nature" that permits man to form private societies and the State "has been instituted to protect and not to destroy natural right . . ." (*Rerum Novarum,* 72). Moreover, the workers may also determine the type of association they wish to have. "Furthermore, if citizens have the free right to associate, they must also have the right freely to adopt the organization and rules which they judge most appropriate to achieve their purpose" (*Rerum Novarum,* 76).

We note that Leo XIII did not use the term "trade unions" in his encyclical. This was not particularly because of a language problem—finding the proper Latin words. It was more a willingness to keep open the question of form and type of associations which the workers might join. Many Catholics who were concerned with the welfare of labour felt that the ideal type of organization would be a joint labour-management group. Some were worried over socialist influence in certain existing labour unions.

The Church accordingly encouraged Catholic workers to form separate unions of their own, or at least to join Christian confessional unions—Protestant-Catholic—that were free from Marxist influence. Nevertheless, it was realized that this request was not always realistic. There were nations in which religiously oriented trade unions would not be practical.

> Under these conditions, Catholics seem almost forced to join secular unions. These unions, however, should always profess justice and equity and give Catholic members full freedom to care for their own consciences and obey the laws of the Church. It is clearly the office of bishops, when they know that these associations are on account of circumstances necessary and not dangerous to religion, to approve of Catholic workers joining them, keeping before their eyes, however, the principles and precautions laid down by Our Predecessor, Pius X, of holy memory. Among these precautions the first and chief is this: side by side with these unions there should always be associations zealously engaged in imbuing and forming their members in the teachings of religion and morality, so that they in turn may be able to permeate the unions with that good spirit which should direct them in all their activity (*Quadragesimo Anno,* 35).

In English-speaking countries, the religiously neutral union has been the rule rather than the exception. In these lands, likewise, there have not been any associations of significant size and influence that would concentrate exclusively on forming workers "in the teachings of religion and morality". The reason for this is evident in our historical chapters. In these lands, cardinals, bishops, and priests intervened at decisive moments when the rights of labour were questioned. Consequently, the unions involved, with some exceptions of those that fell under Communist control, were in no wise opposed to the principles of religion and morality, but rather accepted them willingly.

The general rule in English-speaking nations was to give the workers the same religious formation as was given to other members of the Catholic community. The children of workers went to religious schools or to instruction classes in religion. Workers themselves belonged to parish and diocesan societies without any class distinction. Indeed, many of these workers were immigrants who considered priests who shared a common national origin their closest advisers and counsellors.

These remarks are made without any intent to slight the work of labour schools, associations of Catholic trade unionists, social guilds, Catholic labour colleges, and similar activities largely inspired by the social teaching of the Church. These educational efforts have borne good fruits and have had an influence far beyond the limited numbers of their membership. Such programmes, however, have been primarily positive rather than protective in intent. They aim to disseminate Catholic social principles, rather than to safeguard Catholic workers from allegedly unwholesome influences in secular unions.

There were occasional exceptions to this rule, particularly in the United States and Australia. Catholics concerned with Communist influence or control in certain unions did, at times, organize counter-movements in the attempt to change the political complexion of the unions involved. But these were passing incidents and did not reflect the mainstream of the Catholic response to the labour problem in these countries.

When Pius XII wrote to the bishops of the United States in 1939, he upheld the right of workers to join unions. His only request was that

> the unions in question draw their vital force from principles of wholesome liberty; let them take their form from the lofty rules of justice and of honesty, and, conforming themselves to these norms, let them act in such a manner that in their care for the interests of their class they violate no one's rights; let them continue to strive for harmony and respect the common weal of civil society (*Sertum Laetitiae*).

John XXIII was equally realistic in recognizing that both religious and neutral unions perform useful functions in modern society. In regard to the "Christian associations of workers" he states: "they are fully deserving of our praise. The importance of their work must be gauged not merely by its immediate and obvious results, but also by its effect on the working world as a whole, where it helps spread sound principles of action and the wholesome influence of the Christian religion" (*Mater et Magistra,* 101).

But he also offers words of praise for Catholics who are members of sound secular unions: "We wish further to praise those dear sons of ours who in a true Christian spirit collaborate with other professional groups and workers' associations which respect the natural law and the freedom of conscience of their members" (*Mater et Magistra,* 102). This reaction is typical, not only of Pope John, but also of the traditional attitude of the Holy See towards workers' organizations. Rome recognized that it would be unwise to impose a single uniform pattern on Catholic workers throughout the world, given the wide diversity of national conditions.

CHURCH CRITICISM OF UNIONS

While the Church approves the moral right of workers to organize, it reserves the right to offer counsel and advice when problems arise. This was particularly evident during the pontificate of Pius XII. This pontiff tended to view unions as closely connected with the class struggle. "Unions have arisen as a spontaneous and necessary consequence of capitalism embodied in an economic system. As such the Church gives her approval to them, always with the condition that, depending on the laws of Christ as their unshakable foundation, they endeavour to promote a Christian order in the world of workers" (September 11, 1949). A week earlier he wrote: "May the day be not distant when those organizations of self-defence, which the defects of the hitherto existing economic system and, above all, the lack of Christian mentality have made necessary, could cease to function."

We may contrast this, and other passages from Pius XII to be cited later, with the description of trade unionism given by Pope John XXIII. "Members are no longer recruited in order to agitate, but rather to cooperate, principally by the method of collective bargaining" (*Mater et Magistra*, 97). Within a period of twelve years a different pope reaches a totally different assessment of the labour scene.

The date of the comments by Pius XII gives a possible clue to the reasoning behind the statements. At this time, in Germany, there was strong agitation for labour participation in management. In Belgium a system of industrial councils gave workers a voice in major economic decisions. Pius XII may have felt that this trend would spread and that labour and management would form a team instead of lining up on opposite sides of the class struggle.

There is a note of impatience as well as hope in the passages cited above. It seems clear that there was a period of about ten years—1945-54—in which Pius XII was not exactly happy with trends in unionism as he saw them. This is particularly evident in his Christmas message of 1952. The position taken in this message is of more than routine importance, since this pontiff used his Christmas messages for his major pronouncements.

He notes that

access to employment or places of labour is made to depend on registration in certain parties, or in organizations which deal with the distribution of employment. Such discrimination is indicative of an inexact concept of the proper function of labour unions and their proper purpose, which is the protection of the interests of the salaried workers in modern society, which is becoming more and more anonymous and collectivist.

In fact, is not the essential purpose of unions the practical affirmation that man is the subject, and not the object of social relations? Is it not to protect the individual against collective irresponsibility of anonymous proprietors? Is it not to represent the worker against those who are inclined to consider him merely a productive agent with a certain price value?

How, therefore, can it be considered normal that the protection of the personal rights of the worker be placed more and more in the hands of an anonymous group, working through the agency of immense organizations which are of their very nature monopolies? The worker, thus wronged in the exercise of his personal rights, will surely find especially painful the oppression of his liberty and of his conscience, caught as he is in the wheels of a gigantic social machine.

It is clear that Pius XII felt that at least some segments of labour were falling into the very abuses that were ascribed to employers by earlier popes. They were becoming giant monopolies in which the individual was not only swallowed up, but also oppressed in terms of freedom of conscience. Pius XII speaks in general terms and does not specify in detail the abuses that concern him. Neither does he indicate which unions are involved and what countries deserve this warning.

Judging from social conditions at the time, it is probable that this warning was directed primarily to Germany and secondarily to Belgium, France, and Italy. In Germany, the central labour organization, the DGB, was considered by many of Pius XII's advisers to be under socialist direction. In addition, this union was seeking central appointment of the labour members who were to be on the board of directors and to be labour directors under German codetermination laws. Moreover, socialism and even communism influenced the thinking of many labour leaders in Belgium, France, and Italy. As a result, the major unions tended to be anticlerical if not antireligious. Since these unions in turn exercised considerable political influence, their Catholic members were subject to problems of conscience.

The question has been raised whether or not this passage, and others in papal encyclicals calling for freedom of association, are meant as well to be critical of the closed shop or the union shop which exist in some English-speaking countries. It is possible to reach such a conclusion if these passages are taken apart from their historical contexts. Unless there are compelling reasons to the contrary, the assumption is that the worker should be free to join or not to join a labour association or any similar non-public group.

Even those who hold that a worker has a duty to join a union, as did the bishops of Canada in their pastoral letter of February, 1950, might be reluctant to compel a worker to do this duty. The Canadian bishops argued that unions are necessary to protect family rights and hence that a worker has no right to absent himself from this cause. "In the present state of things, accordingly, there exists a moral obligation to participate actively in one's economic organization." When Pius XI discussed fascist unions in Italy, in which membership was compulsory, he did not condemn this feature (*Quadragesimo Anno,* 91-6). Too much should not be read into this fact, however, since he was deliberately restrained in his appraisal of fascism. In the historical circumstances of the time, he did not deem it appropriate to stir up further trouble.

A better indication that the Holy See has not concerned itself with the union shop is the simple fact that the bishops in the countries which have forms of compulsory unionism have accepted or tolerated this institution as necessary under the circumstances prevailing in their countries. The closed shop and the union shop were adopted as defensive measures to protect the very existence of unions when this was threatened by hostile employers. Workers in effect felt compelled to choose between two principles, both equally valid. The one was the right to form unions and the other was the right to abstain from membership. Those who defend compulsory unionism feel that, in the circumstances, the first principle should prevail.

Normally the Holy See does not intervene in, or pronounce upon, disputes that concern just one or two countries without consulting and informing the bishops involved. To take a hypothetical case, for example, if a pope were contemplating a labour encyclical and this question was referred to him, he might ask a representative group of bishops and theologians in the affected country to give their judgement on the matter. If local opinion is fairly unanimous, Rome is likely to accept the views of those who know the special circumstances prevailing.

THE RIGHT TO STRIKE

Papal references to the right to strike are quite infrequent. Leo XIII said: "Labour which is too long and too hard and the belief that pay is inadequate not infrequently give workers cause to strike and become involuntarily idle. This evil, which is frequent and serious, ought to be remedied by public authority . . ." (*Rerum Novarum,* 56). Pius XII, on June 7th, 1957, told Italian workers "it is better to bargain than to fight one another". To a different group of Italian workers, on June 26th, 1955, he said:

> You are therefore acting in full conformity with the Church's social teaching when, by all means morally permissible, you vindicate your just rights. . . . It is unnecessary to remind you that acts of violence which damage the liberty and goods of others are not even contemplated by Christians. When, therefore, they use the power of their organizations to win recognition for their rights, it is essential that, in the first place, they use the means suitable for negotiation of a peaceful settlement. Then, in particular, there must be taken into consideration whether the results being aimed at are in reasonable proportion to the damage which could result from force.

The bishops of Australia, in 1947, said that "Under modern conditions, the right to organize in trade unions and the right to strike, under certain defined conditions, are inseparable." They listed these conditions, which we shall examine shortly. The bishops of Quebec, in 1950, noted that certain categories of workers perform services so essential that they are forbidden by law to strike. The bishops held that, under these circumstances, there should be compensating methods which are adequate to obtain justice. "The law should, for example, provide for compulsory arbitration, adequately safeguarded in regard to impartiality, effectiveness, and promptness of decision."

When moralists list the conditions that make a strike permissible, they usually give the same rules as those for a just war. These are: a just cause; failure of bargaining and conciliation; expected results proportionate to the sacrifice involved; and the use of lawful and morally sanctioned means.

The first requirement, calling for a just cause, does not mean that only matters of strict justice warrant a strike. Between demands of justice and those that involve injustice there is a wide area of claims based on equity and fairness. If the dispute is over wages, for example, we could say that a strike is just if the employer is making extraordinary profits and paying substandard wages. We would say that a strike is unjust when workers, already paid wages above the industry average, strike for still more and drive an employer to the edge of bankruptcy.

But we might assume a situation in which a living wage is paid by an industry which has had several years of unusually good profits. These profits resulted from better market conditions and not from any increase in efficiency on the part of workers. Is this unusual surplus to be given to stockholders, who are already receiving a good return on their investment, or should the workers also demand a share? Strict justice casts little light on this problem, but there would be a certain fairness and equity in giving the worker a share in these additional returns. One might even justify a short strike to enforce this demand.

Political strikes are in a different category. In a democracy, it is not normal to use economic pressure to secure political demands. Secondary and sympathy strikes also create problems. May workers strike to help their fellows in a competing plant where a strike has already taken place? They may if they have a direct interest in the result, since they may have reason to fear that failure of one group to get its just demands will lead to similar pressures on them later. But it would not be fair to go out just as a demonstration of sympathy, when no direct interest is involved. Jurisdictional strikes often involve problems of justice. They may be permitted when an employer arbitrarily disregards established rules and customs. But they do not seem fair when the employer is the innocent victim of a dispute between two unions.

Finally, there are the cases envisaged by the bishops of Quebec, in which the public interest could not tolerate a strike. Generally speaking, doctors, nurses, firemen, and police should not strike. In cases where a major public inconvenience would be caused, as a strike by bus drivers or garbage collectors, a proportionately grave cause would be required. But when strikes are prohibited, there should be alternate methods for a just settlement of grievances.

A second condition for a morally permissible strike is the use of normal means for settling disputes before a strike is called. There should be a reasonable period of negotiation. If this fails, it is usually proper to call in conciliators to try to mediate the dispute. In most countries today there are both public and private agencies available for such a service.

More questionable is the use of arbitration or labour courts to settle disputes over the negotiation of contracts. No one doubts the value of these devices when used to interpret or enforce a contract previously agreed upon. But they suffer serious deficiencies when used in the negotiation of the claims and interests that arise when a new contract is being discussed. Arbitration is a judicial procedure, whereas claims and interests are not usually matters of strict right.

To cite an example, a union may wish to promote employment in an industry by securing pensions that would permit long-term employees to retire at the age of sixty. It might also ask that workers be given a ten-week vacation after ten years of service. These may be laudable innovations, but a judicial body would be hard put to reach any decision on them. A further difficulty with arbitration is that it entrusts to outsiders decisions that may vitally affect the future of a company. An ill-considered wage increase, for example, might bankrupt the firm. In spite of these limitations, however, compulsory arbitration may be a lesser evil where strikes are forbidden.

The third condition for a strike is that the expected results should be proportionate to the sacrifices involved, not only for the workers, but also for the public. If postal workers were to go on strike because of poor lighting at sorting offices, one would question the wisdom of this decision. Surely there are better ways to acquaint the public with the fact that eyestrain is a problem for these workers.

But, in the intricacies of labour-management relationships, it often happens that an apparently minor matter may involve a major principle. Thus a shop steward may be fined for tardy arrival at a plant. But workers claim that a certain tardiness has always been condoned. They further argue that penalties should not be inflicted without prior warning. Under these conditions, they interpret the fine as an attack on the union itself. They may well strike in order to have the fine revoked.

The final condition is that morally acceptable means be used in the carrying on of a strike. It certainly would be unfair for workers to leave a steel mill, without first taking the steps necessary for a proper cooling of the furnaces. Strikers in a food store should make provision for the orderly sale of perishable goods. No matter how bitter may be the resentment of workers against an employer, it is not legitimate to destroy his machinery or damage his property. Even worse is the use of violence, as may happen when strike-breakers are imported.

A strike is an extremely dangerous weapon, since it affects deeply the economic welfare of both the employer and the workers. Hence it is risky for either side to provoke a walkout without serious cause. There are strikes which are like family quarrels. They let off steam and everyone is better off once the issues are solved. But others are more like blood feuds, in which the hatreds stirred up persist for generations.

Strikes at times seem to be almost like living things with their own rules of inner development. This is particularly true when a strike is prolonged more than a few weeks. In such cases the original disputes are often lost sight of, and a war for survival ensues. Certainly, under these circumstances, it is understandable that the Church should seek to prevent strikes whenever possible. Often her clergy act as mediators of disputes in the effort to prevent suffering and misery. But the most substantial contribution of the Church is her teaching on labour-capital relationships. By eschewing the class struggle and promoting harmony, the Church contributes to the peace and prosperity of peoples. These points will be developed further in the following chapter.

CHAPTER IV

LABOUR

AND MANAGEMENT

This chapter develops at length some of the basic themes discussed at the beginning of our treatment. Since there is a special and unique dignity in each human being, this fact must affect our attitude towards work. It also has profound implications for relationships between labour and management. Papal writings on labour have often stressed the less pleasant aspects of work. Because the toil of millions was long and frequently onerous, the Church reminded workers that this world is both wounded and transitory. It is wounded as a result of original sin and hence we expect to earn our bread in sorrow and suffering. Yet this world will pass away and the tribulations of the moment will bring us imperishable glory in heaven.

Nevertheless, if work can be considered in part a result of the Fall, it also has its creative and redemptive aspects.

> As an indispensable means towards gaining over the world that mastery which God wishes for his glory, all work has an inherent dignity and at the same time a close association with the perfection of the person; this is the noble dignity and privilege of work which is not in any way cheapened by the fatigue and the burden, which have to be borne as the effect of original sin, in obedience and submission to the will of God (Pius XII, Christmas Message, 1942).

This same pope, at Christmas, 1955, noted that:

Man can consider his work as a true instrument of his sanctification because by working he makes perfect in himself the image of God, fulfils his duty and the right to gain for himself and his dependents the necessary sustenance, and makes himself a useful contributor to society. Bringing this order into existence will obtain for him security, and, at the same time the "peace on earth" proclaimed by the angels.

The creative aspect of work naturally varies from occupation to occupation. A craftsman may use his tools to fashion a piece of furniture that is a thing of beauty. But it is also possible that the worker on an automobile assembly line may feel pride in the product which he helped to make. Those who work with other people often feel a real sense of accomplishment. The doctor, nurse, teacher, and social worker can point to the healing and fostering works that they have done.

John XXIII wrote with real eloquence about the spiritual value of farm work.

In the work on the farm the human personality finds every incentive for self-expression, self-development, and spiritual growth. It is a work, therefore, which should be thought of as a vocation, a God-given mission, an answer to God's call to actuate his providential, saving plan in history. It should be thought of, finally, as a noble task, undertaken with a view to raising oneself and others to a higher degree of civilization (*Mater et Magistra*, 149).

PROTECTION OF THE WEAK

Yet it is also possible that work can be performed under conditions that weaken and even debase those involved. One problem is excessive hours of work. When a labourer finds that a job absorbs practically all his waking time and all his energies, he is not living a truly human life. He has no real time to be with his family and to act as father to his children. Long hours of exhausting work are less common today in industrial nations than they were in the time of Leo XIII, yet there are many parts of the world in which debilitating toil is still the rule. As Pius XI observed, too often "dead matter comes forth from the factory ennobled, while men there are corrupted and degraded" (*Quadragesimo Anno,* 135).

Leo XIII had strong words on excessive hours of work. "Assuredly, neither justice nor humanity can countenance the exaction of so much work that the spirit is dulled from excessive toil and that along with the body sinks crushed from exhaustion. The working energy of man, like his entire nature, is circumscribed by definite limits beyond which it cannot go" (*Rerum Novarum,* 59). The pontiff observes that the type of work should affect working hours. For example, miners should have shorter hours than the general norm. Allowance should also be made for severity of climate and for seasons of the year. Health can be affected adversely not only by long hours of work, but also by the conditions under which the work is performed. Extreme heat in a factory is fatiguing. Dust in mines often leads to silicosis. Exposure to rain, snow, and cold can cause pulmonary problems. High noise levels, experienced over many years, lead to deafness. Radioactive materials, smoke, and poisonous gases may also add to industrial hazards.

Some of these conditions may be unavoidable in a technological age, but a worker has the right to every type of protection that is reasonably available. "The conditions in which a man works form a necessary corollary to these rights. They must not be such as to weaken his physical or moral fibre, or militate against the proper development of adolescents to manhood. Women must be accorded such conditions of work as are consistent with their needs and responsibilities as wives and mothers" (*Pacem in Terris,* 19). Years before, Leo XIII said that: "It is not right to demand of a woman or a child what an adult man is capable of doing or would be willing to do. Nay, as regards children, special care ought to be taken that the factory does not get hold of them before age has sufficiently matured their physical, intellectual, and moral powers. . . . Certain occupations likewise are less fitted for women, who are intended by nature for work of the home . . ." (*Rerum Novarum,* 60).

Pius XII upheld the right of women workers to equal pay for equal work.

> Indeed, We have on a former occasion pointed out that for the same work output, a woman is entitled to the same wages as a man. [Yet he deplores the fact that many married women are working:] We see a woman who, in order to augment her husband's earnings, betakes herself to the factory, leaving her house abandoned during her absence. The house, untidy and small perhaps before, becomes even more miserable for lack of care. Members of the family work separately in four corners of the city and with different working hours. Scarcely ever do they find themselves together for dinner or rest after work—still less for prayer in common. What is left of family life? And what attractions can it offer to children? (October 21st, 1945).

In some countries, special groups of workers remain permanently in a disadvantageous position. This is particularly true where there is racial discrimination, oppression of ethnic minorities, or a caste system. The minority group often lives under slum conditions. Children from these groups receive inferior education or none at all. They are denied access to the more skilled and better-paying jobs and this in turn removes incentives to secure a good education. Because of their low incomes their health suffers, as disease and undernourishment take their toll.

In the United States particularly, migratory farm workers are at the bottom of the economic ladder. They work intermittently, often have no permanent home, and may be constantly in debt to the contractors who hire them. This debt leads to virtual slavery, since they are never really free to seek better opportunities. Their children often work in the fields with them. Moreover, the need for constant moving prevents these children from receiving any real education. Since they learn no skills, they are usually condemned to the same fate as that of their parents. A vicious circle of poverty and exploitation persists from generation to generation.

John XXIII was deeply concerned over discrimination based on racial and ethnic differences.

Nor must one overlook the fact that whatever their ethnic background, men possess, besides the special characteristics which distinguish them from other men, other very important elements in common with the rest of mankind. And these can form the basis of their progressive development and self-realization, especially in regard to spiritual values. They have, therefore, the right and the duty to carry on their lives with others in society (*Pacem in Terris,* 100). [He is equally concerned over the plight of political refugees. He finds it impossible to] view without bitter anguish of spirit the plight of those who for political reasons have been exiled from their own homelands. There are great numbers of such refugees at the present time, and many are the sufferings— the incredible sufferings—to which they are constantly exposed (*Pacem in Terris,* 103).

Certainly the human dignity which is the foundation of Catholic social teaching is being outraged by conditions such as those described above. It is thoroughly immoral to treat human beings as mere tools or instruments to be exploited to the limit for the greed and gain of those in power. The glory of the Christian religion has been its recognition of the worth of each individual as a child of God. Working conditions that negate this ideal lead to nothing more than the cruelties of ancient paganism.

HUMAN RELATIONS

What the Church has preached on moral grounds, many industrialists also accept for reasons of psychology or sociology. Pius XII noted this on several occasions.

We are happy to ascertain, nevertheless, that pure technique has vividly brought out the importance, so long ignored, of human relations in labour (February 4th, 1956). [Again] The concern of management is more and more with the men who serve as its collaborators. It is important that these men put forth all their initiative on behalf of the employer. But they will be led to do this only if industry first takes care to fulfil their basic human needs, which are not completely satisfied either by a just salary or even by the appreciation that is due their professional competency (June 10th, 1955).

On another occasion he asserts:

Competent people realize that the worker, when faced with a job which distorts or degrades his personality to the vanishing point, slows down his productive effort and thus reduces considerably the advantages gained twenty-five years ago by mechanization. [He notes that psychologists have tried to study the influences that motivate a worker:] It seems that the most outstanding of these is an active interest in his task, which engages the attention of the man and gives him the feeling of putting his personal resources to work and developing them (January 10th, 1958).

The studies to which Pius XII refers were particularly influential in the last three decades. One of the pioneer studies involved improvement in working conditions, such as better lighting and more pleasant surroundings. This change did lead to increased production. However, much to the surprise of the researchers, the test group maintained its high standards when earlier working conditions were restored. The explanation given was that the fact that these workers were the object of special studies gave them a feeling of importance. Hence they kept up the higher pace of work even when working in an unsatisfactory physical environment. These and related studies indicate that there are untapped resources and energies in the average working force. If proper motivation can be given, workers will be more efficient and productive. There is less danger of waste and spoilage. Sickness and absenteeism tend to decline. Satisfied workers are also less inclined to change jobs, thus reducing the costs involved in training new workers.

Industrial psychologists found flaws in the earlier types of motivation based on piece-work production. It was discovered that an individualistic approach, in which each worker is a competitor to his neighbour, was often unsatisfactory. Workers had a team spirit and resented being forced to compete with their fellows. Hence a better type of incentive system is that which applies to a group as a whole. Researchers also found that the quality of work improves the more that a worker's pride and intelligence are challenged by the job. If he feels that good work is genuinely appreciated, he is more likely to do a good job. When he is consulted and informed about changes, he is much less inclined to resent them and engage in conscious or unconscious sabotage. Thus a new type of industrial relations was brought into being. A foreman would consult with workers and would explain the reasons behind company policy. If major changes were being made, then top management would inform workers why these were necessary. Suggestions were solicited and rewarded. Every effort was made to keep a vigorous two-way communications system between workers and management. At the same time, it was found necessary to avoid any suggestions of artificiality or high-pressure salesmanship. A basic foundation for good industrial relations must be absolute fairness and integrity. Rules must be clear and precise and applied without favouritism or discrimination. Grievances should be settled promptly, with proper machinery for impartial arbitration should the proposed settlement be unsatisfactory.

In effect, these policies led to a form of labour-management partnership. It was not a partnership of complete equality, since management retained its right to make basic decisions. Yet it did involve a high degree of consultation and involvement. It made the worker feel that his human dignity was respected and that he was more than a tool or a cog in a machine.

LABOUR PARTICIPATION IN MANAGEMENT

The process described above involved voluntary action by management. Without denying its merits, it could be said to be selfishly motivated. It might have elements of paternalism. At least, none of the researchers responsible for this new trend claimed that consultation was a matter of right. Indeed, many workers felt that these new developments might be aimed at forestalling union organization, thus depriving workers of a more militant agency for asserting their rights.   .

We have already seen the moral right of workers to organize into unions and to assert their rights through collective bargaining. But do they have any right to participate in management? Some Catholic social scientists argued that they did. Such a view was not accepted by Pius XI.

> Those who declare that a contract of hiring and being hired is unjust of its own nature, and hence a partnership contract must take its place, are certainly in error. . . . We consider it more advisable, however, in the present condition of human society that, so far as it is possible, the work contract be somewhat modified by a partnership contract, as is already being done in various ways and with no small advantage to workers and owners. Workers and other employees thus become sharers in ownership or management or participate in some fashion in the profits received (*Quadragesimo Anno*, 64-5).

Two points are obvious in the material quoted above. Pius XI is not ready to concede any right of workers to participate in management. He upholds the wage contract as morally acceptable. But he gently and cautiously urges that it be modified by elements of partnership, such as sharing in ownership, management, or profits. This is a pastoral exhortation, not a command.

But the position of Pius XI did not quieten those elements that were seeking participation in management as a matter of right. In post-war Germany, the trade union movement was strongly agitating for a law that would give workers an equal number of company directors, serving with those appointed by the stockholders. The unions also demanded the right to appoint the labour-relations director, at least in the iron and steel industry. They got support from the *Katholikentag* of 1948, which declared that the right of comanagement was a natural right.

Pius XII reacted strongly to this declaration. On May 7th, 1949, he declared that: "The owner of the means of production, whoever he may be—individual owner, workers' association or corporation—must always—within the limits of public economic law—retain control of his economic decisions." On June 3rd, 1950, he asserted: "In the light of principles and facts, the right of economic joint-management lies beyond the field of . . . possible achievements."

Once again he addressed himself to this topic on September 14th, 1952:

> The pontiffs of the social encyclicals, and also We ourself, have declined to deduct, directly or indirectly, from the labour contract the right of the employee to participate in the ownership of the operating capital, and its corollary, the right of the worker to participate in the decisions concerning operation of the plant (*Mitbestimmung*). This had to be denied because behind this question there stands that greater problem—the right of the individual and of the family to own property, which stems immediately from the human person. It is a right of personal dignity; a right to be sure accompanied by social obligations; a right, however, not merely a social function.

The key point of papal disagreement concerns the economic functions of management. There would be much less difficulty about asking participation in human-relations areas. But economic decisions involve property ownership, and workers do not have the right to demand control over another's property. In spite of Pius XII's views, German unions did win by law the right of equal representation in the iron and steel industries and minority representation in other firms.

When John XXIII faced this general problem, he did not discuss the German controversy. Rather he approached the problem from the aspect of human dignity and the right of a worker as a human being. The only reference to the earlier controversy was oblique, holding for unity of management. "Obviously, any firm which is concerned for the human dignity of its workers must maintain a necessary and efficient unity of direction." Then he continues: "But it must not treat these employees who spend their days in service with the firm as though they were cogs in the machinery, denying them any opportunity of expressing their wishes or bringing their experience to the work at hand, and keeping them entirely passive in regard to decisions that regulate their activity" (*Mater et Magistra,* 92).

John XXIII's approach is pastoral rather than doctrinal.

> We, no less than our predecessors, are convinced that employees are justified in wishing to participate in the activity of the industrial concern for which they work . . . Every effort must be made to ensure that the enterprise is indeed a true human community, concerned about the needs, the activities, and the standing of each of its members (*Mater et Magistra,* 91).

> [Pope John desires that] the relations between management and employees reflect understanding, appreciation and good will on both sides . . . All this implies that workers have their say in, and make their own contribution to, the efficient running and development of the enterprise (*Mater et Magistra,* 92). [This is particularly true because of recent trends in industrial production.] The present demand for workers to have a greater say in the conduct of a firm accords not only with man's nature, but also with recent progress in the economic, social, and political spheres (*Mater et Magistra,* 93).

As technology advances, greater skill is required of workers. This in turn requires that greater educational and training opportunities should be afforded to these workers. "All this serves to create an environment in which workers are encouraged to assume greater responsibility in their own sphere of employment" (*Mater et Magistra,* 96).

Up to this point, John XXIII does not advance in any way the teaching of his predecessors, although he develops this in more detail and uses more persuasive arguments. The next observations he makes, however, do involve greater recognition of the proper rôle of labour. He notes the development of labour unions in recent times and their tendencies to avoid the class struggle and seek methods of cooperation with management. Consequently these workers should be "given the opportunity to exert their influence throughout the state, and not just within the limits of their own spheres of employment."

The reason for this is that the individual productive concerns, regardless of their size, efficiency, and importance in the state, form but a part—an integral part—of a nation's entire economic and social life, upon which their own prosperity must depend. Hence it is not the decisions within the individual productive units which have the greatest bearing on the economy, but those made by public authorities and by institutions which tackle the various economic problems on a national or international basis. It is therefore very appropriate, or even necessary, that these public authorities and institutions bring the workers into their discussions, and those who represent the rights, demands, and aspirations of the workingmen; and not confine their deliberations to those who merely represent the interests of management (*Mater et Magistra*, 97-9).

Economic decisions by political bodies on a national or international level are public matters, not private actions by the owners of property. Hence workers, and the unions that represent them, participate as a matter of right in deliberations that so deeply affect their welfare. On this level, their interests are co-ordinate with those of management, whereas on the company level workers' claims, while real and substantial, are necessarily subordinate in economic matters.

THE CLASS STRUGGLE

One of the key contributions of Catholic social teaching to the industrial field is its promotion of labour-management harmony rather than the class struggle.

It is a capital evil . . . to take for granted that one class of society is of itself hostile to the other, as if nature had set rich and poor against each other to fight an implacable war . . . the two classes mentioned should agree harmoniously and should properly form equally balanced counterparts to each other. Each needs the other completely: neither capital can do without labour nor labour without capital (*Rerum Novarum*, 28).

[Pius XII asserted:] In the economic domain management and labour are linked in a community of action and interest. . . . Employers and workers are not implacable adversaries.

They are cooperators in a common task. . . . Both parties
are interested in seeing to it that the costs of national production are in proportion to its output. But since the interest is
common, why should it not manifest itself in a common out-
ward expression? (May 7th, 1949)

But the strongest expression came from Pius XI:

In actual fact, human society now, for the reason that it is
founded on classes with divergent aims and hence opposed to
one another and therefore inclined to enmity and strife, continues to be in a violent condition and is unstable and uncer-
tain. But complete cure will not come until this opposition
has been abolished and well-ordered members of the social
body—industries and professions—are constituted in which
men may have their place, not according to the position each
has in the labour market but according to the respective social
functions which each performs (*Quadragesimo Anno,* 82-3).

Pius XI wanted a radical reconstruction of society along
lines which he considered more in accord with human nature
than the present divisions between labour and capital. Both
have important interests in common. Each should be. concerned with the prosperity of the firm and the health of the
national economy. Each wants to abolish poverty and unemployment. Is it not logical for them to work together for such
ends, instead of constantly harping upon factors that divide
them?

This reconstruction of the social order was aimed at much
broader goals than labour-management harmony. It was
hoped that these organized productive bodies would be able
to determine and enforce standards of fair competition and
basic morality in each industry. In this way the burden of
detailed regulation would be lifted from civil society, thereby
permitting the State to concern itself more effectively with
the highest demands of the common good. Pius XI did not
attempt to spell out precise details on this type of social organization. He insisted that the teaching of Leo XIII, that
men are free to choose any form of political government,
provided only that they are concerned with the requirements
of justice and the common good, "is equally applicable in

due proportion, it is hardly necessary to say, to the guilds of the various industries and professions" (*Quadragesimo Anno*, 86).

It was unfortunate that the very sound principles enunciated by Pius XI were often obscured by controversy over their meaning. Some read into them an endorsement of the corporate State, such as exists today in Portugal. Others interpreted them as authorizing extensive and detailed economic planning, of a type commonly associated with communist States. Yet the heart of these proposals does not involve techniques, but rather principles. It is a call for the utmost possible cooperation in economic society and the hope that suitable structures can be evolved to give this cooperation stability and permanence. Within the framework of these principles, individual nations and peoples will develop methods in accordance with their history and culture. Such developments will receive the blessing of the Catholic Church.

CHAPTER V

POVERTY

AND UNEMPLOYMENT

In spite of the efforts of organized labour and social-minded employers, we must face the fact that poverty is very much a part of modern life. Three particular types of destitution are significant in the modern world. There is a type that prevails throughout an entire nation. Many of the developing nations in Asia, Africa, and Latin America can be characterized as substantially poor. In these cases there is little in the form of national product to be distributed. Another type of poverty can be classed as regional. In nations otherwise well off there are areas of declining production or sections which have never developed economically. Poor soil, lack of suitable communications, and inadequate education may explain these pockets of want. Mines or forests may be depleted. Perhaps excessive specialization in one type of industry led to tragedy when markets for this product declined or even vanished.

A third form of poverty involves certain classes or groups in a population. Slum conditions, for reasons which Pius XII explains later, often tend to be self-perpetuating. Unskilled workers are less and less in demand in the modern world, so that consequently many are either unemployed or poorly paid. Racial and ethnic discrimination can be factors leading to want. In some countries there is a prejudice against hiring older workers, even workers over forty. Often farmers seem to find themselves at the bottom of the economic ladder. The common thread in all these cases is the fact that such poverty seems to persist in wealthy nations, and that it is often unresponsive to the ameliorating influence even of sustained general prosperity.

Finally, the fact of unemployment is relevant to poverty. Surprisingly it is not a major cause in many nations. But sustained joblessness can exhaust savings, unemployment compensation, and similar last-resort sources of sustenance. And it is damaging to the morale of workers, so that they may be less fit for work when it becomes available.

Each of these problems has been noted by the popes of the social encyclicals. We shall study them in some detail in the present chapter, not only giving the reactions of the Holy See to the problems outlined, but also trying to integrate proposed remedies with the general body of Catholic social teaching as outlined in earlier chapters. Before going into these details, we shall offer some observations on the general problem of poverty. We may use here, without quotation marks, material contributed to the NCWC Social Action Department statement, "A Religious View of Poverty."

THE CHURCH AND POVERTY

There is paradox in the Christian teaching on poverty. Our Lord called the poor blessed, yet he praised highly those who helped the hungry, the homeless, the unclothed. St Paul said that God has chosen "the things that are not, to bring to naught the things that are; lest any flesh should pride itself before him" (I Cor. 1. 29). St James declared: "Has not God chosen the poor of this world to be rich in faith and heirs of the kingdom which God has promised to those who love him" (James 2. 5).

The Church has endorsed poverty by demanding it from those who enter the religious life under solemn vows. These give up the right to use and dispose of worldly goods. They do this, not because the world that God made is evil, but in order to cut their ties with all that might turn their gaze from God and lead them to concentrate on the passing and corruptible. Yet, and herein lies the paradox of the Christian teaching on poverty, the Church also speaks of a form of poverty that hurts the soul, something totally different from religious detachment from worldly goods. There is a destitution that binds men to this earth, since it forces them to use every waking moment to keep body and soul together. There is want that breeds bitterness and resentment, even hatred.

Pius XII, in his Christmas message of 1952, spoke of

the consequences of poverty, still more of the consequences of utter destitution. For some families there is a dying daily, a dying hourly; a dying multiplied, especially for parents, by the number of dear ones they behold suffering and wasting away . . . sickness becomes more serious, because it is not properly treated; it strikes little ones in particular, because preventive measures are lacking. Then there is the weakening and consequent physical deterioration of whole generations. Whole masses of the population are brought up as enemies of law and order. . . . [This poverty often leads to] social conditions which, whether one wills it or not, make difficult or practically impossible a Christian life (June 1st, 1941). [These poor live in] dilapidated, ramshackle houses without the most necessary hygienic installations. . . . Enough cannot be said about the harm that these dwellings do to the families condemned to live in them. Deprived of air and light, living in filth and in unspeakable commingling, adults and above all children quickly become the prey of contagious diseases which find a favourable soil in their weakened bodies. But the moral injuries are still more serious: immorality, juvenile delinquency, the loss of taste for living and working, interior rebellion against a society that tolerates such abuses, ignores human beings, and allows them to stagnate in this way, transformed gradually into wrecks (May 2nd, 1957).

In some cases, poverty may spring from individual disability of the type that cannot readily be remedied. Here we think of aged persons, particularly those whose savings have been used up because of serious illness. There are also persons who are physically and mentally handicapped. Some mothers are the sole support of young children and cannot work without injury to these children. In all these cases the answer is the compassionate charity preached by the Lord and practised in various ways by his followers throughout the centuries. But in many other cases, poverty springs primarily from social conditions. Millions throughout the world have the ability and desire for work, but are unable to find suitable employment. Some are idle. Others, because of lack of training, or various forms of discrimination or exploitation, have employment but do not receive wages adequate for decent living. Here we have a challenge to the social conscience of the Christian. We shall now examine how various popes have expressed this challenge.

EMPLOYMENT FOR ALL

Pius XI wrote his encyclical "On Reconstructing Social Order" at a time when a serious economic depression gripped most of the industrial world. Unemployment was widespread. Understandably he could stress that "opportunity to work be provided for those who are able and willing to work". He noted that wages and salaries affect employment. "For everyone knows that an excessive lowering of wages, or their increase beyond due measure, causes unemployment." There should be a "right proportion among wages and salaries" and also "in the prices at which goods are sold that are produced by the various occupations, such as agriculture, manufacturing, and others. If all these relations are properly maintained, the various occupations will combine and coalesce into, as it were, a single body and like members of the body mutually aid and complete one another" (*Quadragesimo Anno,* 74-5).

Pius XII notes that "efforts must be made to attain the highest possible level of employment, but at the same time means must be sought to ensure its stability". He hopes that this can be done by private industry, but states that "where private initiative is inactive or inadequate, the public authorities are obliged to provide employment, so far as possible, by undertaking works of general utility, and to facilitate by counselling and other means the finding of employment by those who seek it" (Christmas, 1952). In seeking for full employment, we should not neglect "to prevent the risk of inflation" (September 9th, 1956).

When the popes write about highly technical problems, such as unemployment, they are primarily concerned with the moral aspects of these problems. They pass judgement upon the human impact of such developments and set goals which the economy should seek. If, in the course of their presentation, they mention the accepted theories of their day as to the cause and the remedies for the situation, this is not an exercise of their religious teaching authority.

Thus when Pius XI wrote about wage and price distortions as being the prime causes of unemployment, and called for balance among these factors in order to bring about abundant production, he was using the tools of economic theory available to him at the time. Later, John Maynard Keynes was to write his celebrated study of employment and to conclude that it is possible to achieve economic balance at a level that leaves men and resources unemployed. Many of his followers paid little attention to structural distortions as factors in economic decline, and held that money management and public investment should be the prime weapons against both unemployment and economic slippage. At the present moment, leading economists tend to give about equal weight to both factors. They feel that industry and labour should avoid price and wage distortions, inflation, excessive inventories accumulated to protect against the threat of inflation, dangerous speculation in the securities markets, and other excesses that could seriously affect major industries or even the whole economy.

Yet, at the same time, they are aware of the overwhelming impact of factors which are largely under the control of central governments. Thus the bank rate for loans can usually be influenced by national policy, especially by central-bank and treasury decisions. Low interest rates stimulate borrowing and economic expansion, whereas higher rates have a braking effect. Tax policies likewise can either stimulate or restrain business activity. Again there is the tremendous impact on the economy of a budget surplus or deficit in a national government. A surplus is deflationary and a deficit inflationary.

Hence the range of tools available to fight unemployment is much greater than was known to Pius XI or possibly even to Pius XII. Economic balance and public works are but two of many diverse approaches to this intricate problem. It is evident that John XXIII was quite aware of this increasing complexity of economic life (see *Mater et Magistra,* 54). Because of this knowledge, he was more willing than his predecessors to urge positive governmental steps to secure stability and growth and to level social inequalities.

AUTOMATION

Pius XII spoke frequently about automation in addresses given during the year 1957. On the one hand he realized that many benefits will be secured from this drastic breakthrough in productive techniques and capacity.

> Now, if it is true that in the early stages the machine often enslaved man, who was supposed to control it, today machine tools have been perfected to a point where one can hope that an ever-increasing number of workers will be free who have until now been subjected to the performance of purely material and monotonous tasks. (October 23rd) [Again] it is also foreseen that the age of automation will constantly reassert the pre-eminence of intellectual values among the productive class: knowledge, ingenuity, organization, foresight (March 7th).

> [But he also has many cautions to offer:] There is no doubt that the period of transition may result in an increase of unemployment among older workers, who are less adapted to new training, but younger labourers as well are faced with the same danger whenever a nation is forced to hasten its steps towards automation because of its competition with other countries. This is why it is necessary to make suitable plans, starting now, so that the dynamism of technology may not

result in public calamity. In every case producers must accept
the principle that technology is at the service of the economy,
and not *vice versa* (March 7th).

Later in 1957 he noted the danger of confusing technical
productivity with economic productivity. Automation leads to
a fantastic growth in productive capacities. But will it lead to
"a lasting and sure attainment of conditions which will make
possible the material and human well-being of every member
of the population, and in which all those who contribute immediately—with their labour, their property, their capital—to
the national economy will receive a return corresponding to
their investment"? (June 7th)

Pius XII is aware of the arguments that in the long run
employment will rise as a result of automation. But even if
this were true, "the fact remains that an increase in technological unemployment even for a brief period would represent in some countries a loss that could not be lightly
incurred. In this area it is not at all legitimate to adopt the
false principle which in the past impelled certain statesmen
to sacrifice an entire generation in view of the great advantages that would accrue to succeeding ones" (June 7th).

An authoritative treatment of automation is found in the
letter sent by Cardinal Cicognani to the Canadian Social
Week on behalf of John XXIII. It points out that:

> it is, therefore, a requirement of social justice that such ap-
> plication [of automation] be made in such a way that the
> immediate negative results should not be borne exclusively by
> workers or by certain groups of workers. Rather such negative
> results should weigh equally, or even more heavily, upon the
> investors of capital and, when appropriate, even upon all
> members of the political community, since all in the final
> analysis benefit by such changes of automation. This can
> the more surely be obtained when the workers, through their
> unions and organizations, are present and have a voice in the
> implementation of the processes of automation (October 16th,
> 1961).

This letter further suggests that workers be prepared to
assume higher responsibilities as required by automated

production. This calls for better education and for training programmes sponsored by labour and management. Cardinal Cicognani feels that such activities may be appropriate for organizations of the lay apostolate.

As a social phenomenon, automation must be considered as one of the major developments of recent decades. At first there was a tendency to underestimate its impact and to consider it on a par with technological changes of earlier years. More recently the pendulum of thought has swung to the opposite extreme and some persons despair of ever finding jobs for the workers who will ultimately be displaced by the new processes. Whether or not this despairing attitude is justified, it is clear that the facile assumptions of a few years back lack validity. Automation is not like the introduction of the automobile, which displaced the horse and carriage and related service industries, only to create millions of new jobs directly or indirectly related to motor transport. In some fields at least automation is moving decisively in the direction of displacing far more workers than can be absorbed either by expanded production in the automated industry or by occupations incidental to the process of automation.

Nor is it clear that displaced workers can readily be retrained so as to find jobs in other occupations or even other areas of a nation. Some workers are too old to profit by retraining. Others may lack the talents for occupations which still need workers. Undoubtedly over the years there will be a shift of employment from agriculture, mining, and manufacturing to service industries which are less affected by technology. But nations which need doctors, nurses, social workers, and teachers are not likely to recruit them from industrial or farm workers displaced by recent trends.

One of Cardinal Cicognani's suggestions, that investors bear part of the social cost of automation, will meet with a mixed reception in most nations. Many firms are willing to seek to retrain or reassign workers whose jobs are automated. Others agree not to discharge any workers, rather relying upon retirement and resignations to bring the work force down to a lower level. This approach does help older employed workers, but it gives no answer to the problem of younger workers who cannot find jobs.

It is not our function here to give an economic or political analysis of the problem, but rather to emphasize the Church's teaching on matters relating to labour. It is clear from the quotations given that the Church does not believe that this problem will solve itself. The affected parties, labour, management and government, must give extended study to the issues involved and earnestly seek solutions that will safeguard human values, the while enjoying the economic benefits of technology.

REGIONS OF DECLINING INDUSTRY

The prevalence of uneven development of regions and resources within a nation is likewise a source of unemployment and poverty. "Among citizens of the same political community there is often a marked degree of economic and social inequality. The main reason for this is that they are living and working in different areas, some of which are more economically developed than others. Where this situation obtains, justice and equity demand that public authority try to eliminate or reduce such imbalances" (*Mater et Magistra,* 150).

In this connection we think of the coal regions of the United Kingdom and the United States and the problems of the South of Italy. In the United States, indeed, the entire Appalachian region has been designated as a poverty area. Not only is there a mining problem in this area, but it is also characterized by farms whose productive capacities are quite low.

John XXIII has a number of broad suggestions for meeting the problem of depressed areas. Public authority

should ensure that the less developed areas receive such essential public services as their circumstances require, in order to bring the standard of living in these areas into line with the national average. Furthermore, a suitable economic and social policy must be devised which will take into account the supply of labour, the drift of population, wages, taxes, credit, and the investing of money especially in expanding industries. In short, it should be a policy designed to promote useful employment, enterprising initiative, and the exploitation of local resources (*Mater et Magistra,* 150).

In the past, migration has often been the "natural" solution to the problems just outlined. Younger and better educated workers go where opportunities are greater to seek their livelihood. If there are labour shortages in other regions or even nations, as happened in Europe in the 1960's, there is often active recruiting of workers from less developed areas. But such measures are not entirely satisfactory, since they force workers to leave their native areas and live among strangers, even going to lands in which a different language is spoken.

Much better, where feasible, are plans to attract industry into places in which there are idle workers or families living in poverty. Generous tax credits and even the subsidizing of factory buildings may attract new firms, as Ireland and Puerto Rico demonstrate. At times the availability of roads or other forms of transport permit the development of tourist industry in wilder regions not suitable for manufacturing, mining or agriculture. These activities should not be carried on in a spirit of paternalism. Rather "everything must be done to insure that citizens of the less developed areas are treated as responsible human beings, and are allowed to play the major rôle in achieving their own economic, social, and cultural development" (*Mater et Magistra,* 151). Finally, John XXIII insists that private enterprise must be given a suitable share in this process. Public authority should assist private firms, in accordance with the principle of subsidiarity. New development should also be balanced, with agriculture, industry, and the services being promoted simultaneously.

AID TO DEVELOPING NATIONS

There is a close similarity between the problems of depressed areas and those faced by less developed nations. Living standards are low, poverty is endemic, and often there is serious unemployment or underemployment. Yet there are also important differences, chief of which is the fact that the developing nations are independent States, not subdivisions of a larger political community. Many of them have no cultural or strong political ties with wealthier nations, although some former colonies have maintained close connections with the onetime colonial power.

Where customary ties are lacking between wealthy and impoverished nations, we must establish such connections on the basis of the moral unity of mankind. "The solidarity which binds all men together as members of a common family makes it impossible for wealthy nations to look with indifference upon the hunger, misery, and poverty of other nations whose citizens are unable to enjoy even elementary human rights. . . . It is necessary to educate one's conscience to the sense of responsibility which weighs upon each and every one, especially upon those who are more blessed with this world's goods" (*Mater et Magistra,* 157-8).

To do this, wealthy nations must provide those in need with the scientific, technical, and professional training they require. They should also put at their disposal the necessary capital for speeding up their economic development with the help of modern methods. The pope blesses international and regional organizations that are working towards this goal. He notes with pleasure that thousands of young men and women are being given the opportunities to attend universities in more developed lands. Thus they can acquire up-to-date technical, scientific, and professional training. He praises "world banking institutes" as well as individual States and private persons who furnish capital "for an ever richer network of economic enterprises in less wealthy countries." He calls this a magnificent work. "It is a work, however, which needs to be increased, and we hope that the years ahead will see the wealthier nations making even greater efforts for the scientific, technical, and economic advancement of those political communities whose development is only in its initial stages" (*Mater et Magistra,* 165).

He asks only that developing nations be careful to secure a proper balance between industry, agriculture, and the services. They should distribute wealth fairly among all members of the community. And they should not blindly copy the cultural characteristics of wealthier nations, but rather preserve the best elements of their own culture. Aiding nations in turn should respect this individuality.

The economics of aid to developing nations have not been fully worked out at this time. Nations like individuals tend to have their own character and inner dynamism. Under apparently identical economic and social conditions, some peoples prosper and others lag behind. Even the same peoples react differently at different times. In present-day Europe, for example, such countries as Italy, Greece, Ireland and Spain are beginning to move forward rapidly after centuries of comparative poverty. Even behind the boundaries of the communist world, we find Yugoslavia and Rumania beginning to move forward much more rapidly than their comrades in the so-called socialist camp of nations.

These points are noted, not in any way to downplay John XXIII's exposition of common human goals, but rather to stress the complexity of the problem to be faced. Nations which take the simplistic and naïve view that a certain amount of training and investment will automatically work wonders in poorer lands often end up discouraged and disillusioned. Intelligent and carefully thought out programmes of foreign aid are more likely to bring enduring results and hence are more likely to be maintained over a prolonged period of time.

Again it is not our function to delve into the economics of this problem. Our aim rather is to illustrate and clarify the principles so well expressed by John XXIII, by noting the wide variations that will be found in the countries which receive such aid. In this way, we can approach the political problem which wealthier nations often face when confronted by what seem to be endless demands for overseas assistance. The more clearly and forcefully citizens, inspired by the social teaching of the Church, express their convictions in plausible political terms, the more likely it is that such aid will be forthcoming to those in need.

CHAPTER VI

SOCIAL LEGISLATION

In our historical discussion of Catholic social action, there are frequent references to demands for social legislation. Government intervention was considered necessary in order to protect the rights of workers, and particularly to safeguard women and children. More than this, Catholic leaders were often in the forefront, especially in Germany and France, in securing the passage of protective statutes.

Leo XIII urged that public authorities safeguard the rights of workers.

> Rights indeed, by whomsoever possessed, must be religiously protected; and public authority, in warding off injuries and punishing wrongs, ought to see to it that individuals may have and hold what belongs to them. In protecting the rights of private individuals, however, special consideration must be given to the weak and the poor. For the nation, as it were, of the rich is guarded by its own defences and is in less need of governmental protection, whereas the suffering multitude, without the means to protect itself, relies especially on the protection of the State. Wherefore, since wage workers are numbered among the great mass of the needy, the State must include them under its special care and foresight (*Rerum Novarum,* 54).

Leo XIII does utter one word of caution, holding that "the law ought not to undertake more, nor should it go further, than the remedy of evils or the removal of dangers requires" (*Rerum Novarum,* 53). This is in accord with the principle of subsidiarity. Excessive or extreme State intervention leads to undue centralization of political power and the danger of statism. When Pius XI discusses this problem, he is more specific in terms of the protection offered. "These laws undertake the protection of life, health, strength, family, homes, workshops, wages, and labour hazards, in fine, everything which pertains to the condition of wage workers, with special concern for women and children" (*Quadragesimo Anno,* 28). He feels that much credit must be given to *Rerum Novarum* for these laws, even though they may not completely reflect the spirit of this encyclical.

His successor, Pius XII, also returned to this theme, but with certain qualifications and hesitations. He noted that in several nations,

> often under the decisive influence of the Catholic social movement, social policy has been taking the form of a progressive evolution in labour legislation, with a corresponding subjection of the private owner of the means of production to juridical obligations in favour of the workingman. The desire to see social policy further developed along these lines encounters a limit, and that limit is reached where the danger arises that the working class may follow in its turn the mistaken course of capital. That course involved the withdrawing of personal responsibility, chiefly in big business, from the private owner (individual or partnership) and handing it over to the responsibility of anonymous corporate groups (June 3rd, 1950).

The reference here to big business concerns the separation of ownership and control in the modern corporation. In large firms, stock ownership is so diffused that the individual stockholder is unable to exercise the slightest control over the policies of the company, even though nominally he is an owner. Pius XII felt that a further increase in social legislation in Europe would so concentrate power in the State that workers would ultimately suffer. It would lead to socialism by removing from private property its function of "stimulating initiative and fixing responsibility in economic matters" (*Ibid.*).

This same pontiff again expressed his concern in a later address. He insisted that the Church "opposes, on the basis of moral principles, everyone who would attribute to the State excessive control over the economic life of its citizens". In particular he was against "total planning". The results of such a policy are disastrous: "The just liberties of the individual are destroyed. The serenity of labour is disturbed. The sacred character of the family is violated. The love of country is corrupted. The precious patrimony of religion is obliterated." Lest this stand be misunderstood, he continues: "Our rejection of totalitarian planning which destroys all individual enterprise does not imply that a regime of absolute freedom in the economic world is acceptable. This would in fact set a premium on indifference to the welfare of others, and would engender contempt for certain indispensable principles dictated by considerations of human and Christian brotherhood" (April 13th, 1956).

We have noted before how changed social conditions often lead to a shift of emphasis in papal teaching. When Pius XII seemed to call a halt to further social legislation, he was not setting himself at variance with his predecessors. What had been done thus far, he approved, at least in broad outlines. But he greatly feared that labour was pushing its demands for protection too far, and was approaching the point at which private property and free initiative would be badly impaired, if not destroyed.

Pius XII had good reasons to be concerned over excessive centralization of power. He had to suffer the agonies of world War II, caused by the overweening ambition of leaders of two totalitarian States. After the war, he saw the forces of Soviet Communism fill the power vacuum in Eastern Europe and threaten the entire world. In economic life, he feared that big business would stamp out small owners and independent proprietors, thus leading to further concentration of power even within democratic nations. He judged that labour in turn was reacting to these trends by demanding more and more State intervention. As bitter experience showed him, extreme concentration of power is destructive of the vital freedoms which all men should cherish.

JOHN XXIII ON SOCIAL LEGISLATION

John XXIII did not share completely these fears concerning State intervention. Moreover, he seemed more conscious than any previous pope of the wide diversity of conditions throughout the world. He was less inclined to permit purely European developments to colour his outlook on current society. It is significant that, in summarizing the teachings of his predecessors, he is almost completely silent about the issues that worried Pius XII. Even when John XXIII touches on similar problems, he is more likely to be positive in his approach. Thus he would stress the positive values of individual initiative and private property rather than dwell at length on dangers of excessive State power.

His treatment of the powers and duties of government has more of the tone of Leo XIII and Pius XI than the more worried approach of Pius XII. He holds, for example, that the State "cannot hold aloof from economic matters. On the contrary, it must do all in its power to promote the production of a sufficient supply of material goods. . . . It has also the duty to protect the rights of all its people, and particularly of its weaker members, the workers, women, children. It can never be right for the State to shirk its obligation of working actively for the condition of the working-man" (*Mater et Magistra*, 20). He notes specifically that terms of employment should be regulated in accordance with justice and equity. And the State should see that working conditions are compatible with the human dignity of workers.

We noted in the previous chapter that John XXIII was well aware of the tremendous economic power of the modern State. This enables it to reduce imbalances in the economy, whether these involve depressed areas or uneven development of one type of activity, such as agriculture. Modern trends give "public authority a greater means for limiting fluctuations in the economy and for providing effective measures to prevent the recurrences of mass unemployment" (*Mater et Magistra*, 54).

While all this impels public authorities to increase the degree and scope of their activities in the economic sphere, it should never lead to policies which deprive the individual citizen of his freedom of action. The ideal is mutual co-operation in these matters between individual citizens and the State: "Both sides must work together in harmony, and their respective efforts must be proportioned to the needs of the common good in the prevailing circumstances and conditions of human life" (*Mater et Magistra*, 56; see also *Pacem in Terris*, 56-7).

Failure of government to be vigilant can lead to distressing results. We know that "in the modern world especially, political, economic, and cultural inequalities among citizens become more and more widespread when public authorities fail to take appropriate action in these spheres. And the consequence is that human rights and duties are thus rendered totally ineffective" (*Pacem in Terris*, 63).

To carry out these aims

the public administration must give considerable care and thought to the question of social as well as economic progress, and to the development of essential services in keeping with the expansion of the productive system. Such services include road-building, transport, communications, drinking-water, housing, medical care, ample facilities for the practice of religion, and aids to recreation. The government must also see to the provision of insurance facilities, to obviate any likelihood of a citizen's being unable to maintain a decent standard of living in the event of some misfortune, or greatly increased family responsibilities (*Pacem in Terris*, 64).

Other matters considered suitable for government action, John XXIII notes, include helping workers to find employment in keeping with their aptitudes, a wage based on justice and equity, giving workers a sense of responsibility in the industrial concerns for which they work, and the formation of intermediate groups in society, so that the social life of the people may become more fruitful and less constrained.

This enumeration of activities considered to be the duty of government involves a very considerable intervention in the economy. There are modern nations in which such proposals would be considered highly controversial. Thus Canada and the United States have had acrimonious disputes about government provisions for medical care. Public housing is not always accepted in certain areas of the United States. Nor does this powerful nation have a social insurance system as comprehensive as that taken for granted by John XXIII. There might be disputes over government action to secure proper wages (in contrast to minimum wages) and to give workers a part of the responsibility in industrial organizations.

We make these observations, not in terms of special pleading for more extensive government activities in the economic sphere, but rather to afford perspective when issues of public policy are being debated. Particularly in the United States of America there is a tendency on the part of some polemicists to use the labels socialism and communism indiscriminately. The growing intervention of public authority in economic matters—a trend which John XXIII seems to take for granted—is often described in public debates as creeping socialism. Persons who are not well versed in history or aware of social developments in other lands can be misled into believing that certain proposals are pure Marxism, whereas in other democratic countries they are considered necessary elements of public policy.

In the following pages, we shall discuss specific types of social legislation and government activity designed to help the worker and particularly those who are poor and defenceless.

HOUSING

Pius XII was deeply concerned over the problem of housing. He insisted:

The Catholic Church strongly supports the requirements of social justice. These requirements include provision for the people of the necessary houses, and above all for those who desire to found a family or are already doing so. Can there be conceived a social need of greater urgency? (July 24th, 1949). [On another occasion, after a vivid description of the evils of slum living, he concludes:] Society itself must bear the consequences of this lack of foresight. Because it did not wish to prevent the evil and to provide a remedy in time, it will spend enormous sums to keep up an appearance of curbing delinquency and to pay expenses for prolonged confinement in sanatoriums and clinics. How many millions are authorized for the cure of evils that it would have been easier and less expensive to prevent! (May 3rd, 1957). [However, this does not of itself mean that public housing is the primary answer:] Public authorities should, in regard to housing, as in other matters, seek to favour, and in no case oppose, private enterprise. In the case of popular housing especially, they should favour the enterprise of cooperatives (November 21st, 1953).

We know from experience that government, working together with private industry, can do much to provide good housing. Zoning and building codes, for example, can help prevent the creation of slum areas. There can be requirements for certain facilities and space for a given number of persons. Landlords can be compelled to make needed repairs and to furnish essential services, such as the providing for adequate heating. Building inspectors can be alert for fire and health hazards.

Where slums do exist and are beyond any reasonable hope of repair, public authorities may take over title to the land and property and tear down dilapidated buildings. The land can then be sold to private builders, often with tax concessions designed to promote limited-income housing. Government can also help by making loans available to private persons who wish to erect good houses. Or it can guarantee mortgages made by banks and other lending firms. Cooperatives can be formed to assist in securing low-cost housing.

All this, however, may not be sufficient in the case of the very poor. They simply have not the income to own or rent private housing that is adequate in space and quality. The overcrowding that is characteristic of slums reflects this fact, since entire families may be forced to live in one or two rooms. Under these conditions, one of two methods might be used to secure adequate living space for such needy persons. It would be possible for public authorities to pay part of the rent for suitable private housing for the poor. Or they can construct public housing facilities, setting the rent according to the ability of the family to pay, rather than on a commercial basis of offsetting costs. Those who are concerned over the cost of such measures might reflect on the far greater social costs of slums, with their high crime and disease rate. Even if we are indifferent to the sufferings of the poor, we might realize that it is better to spend public funds for good housing than to be taxed for enormous police forces and huge prison institutions.

SOCIAL SECURITY

At Christmas, 1950, Pius XII proclaimed "the fight against unemployment and the striving after a sound social security as an indispensable condition if all members of a nation, both high and low, are to be united in a single corporate body". Some years later, he discussed the matter more at length:

> Undoubtedly, nowadays more than in the past, there is a growing desire to assure to all classes of society guarantees that will preserve them from mishaps and chances inherent in the fluctuations of the economy; guarantees that will protect employment and its rewards; guarantees that will provide for sickness and incapacitating accidents that may reduce a man to idleness and deprive him of the means of livelihood. This solicitude is quite justified; but in many cases the present system of social security has not yet succeeded in putting an end to difficult situations or in healing wounds that are always open.
>
> It is important, however, that the anxious desire for security should not prevail over the businessman's readiness to risk his resources to such an extent as to dry up every creative im-

pulse; nor impose on enterprise operating conditions that are
too burdensome; nor discourage those who devote their time
and energy to commercial transactions (February 17th, 1956).

John XXIII discusses social insurance in the context of
agricultural problems, but he advances to principles that are
broadly applicable to all elements of society. He holds, for
example, that the fact that farm workers have lower incomes than other workers is no reason why their social-
insurance allowances should be substantially smaller.

Insurance programmes that are established for the general
public should not differ markedly whatever be the economic
sector in which the individuals work or have their source of
income. Systems of social insurance and social security can
make a most effective contribution to the overall distribution
of income in accordance with the principles of justice and
equity. They can therefore be instrumental in reducing imbalances between the different classes of citizens (*Mater et
Magistra*, 135-6).

These observations of John XXIII's are extremely important, since they move in the direction of a concept that is
likely to gain increasing favour throughout the world. It is
simply stated: no human being should be deprived of goods
and services essential for his welfare, merely because an
imperfect economic system failed to provide him with the
opportunity to earn sufficient income. Persons who, for
reasons of age, sickness, handicaps, and similar disabilities
are unable to work, should be assured proper housing, clothing, food, medical care and similar necessities. Those who
are unemployed, or whose jobs do not give them adequate
income, should be furnished supplemental income from society, so that they also will be able to enjoy the necessities of
life.

Existing social-security and social-assistance programmes
do furnish such security in most industrial nations in the
modern world. But often the coverage is inadequate and in-
complete. There may be areas in which such assistance is
given under conditions which the recipients find humiliating

and degrading. In some countries there is still the conscious or unconscious assumption that poverty, unemployment and similar difficulties are necessarily the fault of the individual. It is taken for granted that anyone with proper qualities of character ought to be able to provide for himself and for his dependants.

This may well have been the case in simpler agrarian societies. Under such conditions, even those who were blind, crippled or otherwise unable to work were taken care of by relatives. Idleness and extreme poverty, in these circumstances, might be considered as indicating laziness and lack of suitable thrift. In Anglo-Saxon countries the Puritan ethic tended to reinforce this attitude.

But in the modern world very few families can live off the land, feeding, clothing, and housing themselves from the bounty of the earth. Our economic system today is highly specialized. Individuals can earn income only by finding a suitable niche in this system. Fortunately most of them are successful in doing this. Nevertheless, it is quite possible that economic life will go on in a prosperous fashion, distributing abundance to a great majority of citizens, yet having no suitable place for an unfortunate minority. Some lack work; others cannot earn enough at work to rise above the level of poverty.

A situation such as this might be considered anomalous by the traditional visitor from Mars. Nations are plagued with surpluses of food, while many of their citizens are undernourished or even hungry. Factories run at less than capacity at a time when millions lack suitable medicines, clothing, and housing. Automation multiplies our capacity to produce, but often gives no answer to the problem of how men are to earn incomes so they can buy these products. No wonder John XXIII asserted that "systems of social insurance and social security can make a most effective contribution to the overall distribution of income in accordance with the principles of justice and equity" (*Mater et Magistra,* 136).

At the present time, five general categories of social insurance are common in the modern world. These are old-age, invalidity, and survivors' insurance; health and maternity insurance; family allowances; work-injuries insurance; and unemployment insurance. Not all of these are insurance in the strict sense of the term, at least if we consider protection against unforeseen risks as a prime element in insurance. Old-age pensions, for example, are savings rather than insurance programmes. But the term insurance is widely used to cover all the five categories listed above.

Old-age and survivors' benefits are very common in the modern world because of changed conditions of society. In a simpler, more agrarian, society it was possible for children generally to take care of their aged parents. There was room for them in the home, and indeed they were able to make a contribution to the maintenance and operation of the household. This is not always feasible in the crowded cities of our age. Nor is it easy for most workers to save enough to live in complete independence upon their retirement. Whether we like it or not, there are strong social pressures today which lead most persons of average means to spend the bulk of their incomes. Only the comparatively well off find it possible to save sizable amounts for old age.

Health insurance is still considered a controversial topic in many parts of the world. At the same time there are complaints that the costs of private medical treatment and hospital care can be considerable burdens. The very advances of modern medicine, with its complex drugs and intricate diagnostic and therapeutic equipment, make it almost impossible to finance certain types of care from current income and normal savings. Some combination of prepayment and insurance is needed to take care of both routine treatment and catastrophic illness. More and more the modern world is turning to some variety of health insurance, often public in nature, to meet these pressing needs.

Family allowances are available in over sixty nations in the world today. Programmes differ from country to country, with some nations gearing the benefits in such a way as to promote large families, and others seeking to discourage families over a certain size. Regardless of techniques used, a strong economic and moral case can be made for family allowances. From the economic viewpoint, it has about the same effect as grading wages according to need. This is certainly better than trying to pay every worker, regardless of marital status and number of dependants, an amount sufficient to support a family. The moral case hardly needs arguing.

Workingmen's compensation for injuries is one of the oldest types of social insurance and also it is almost universally adopted today in industrial nations. It is hard to believe that, at the time of Leo XIII, most workers had no recourse, no matter how they were injured at work. Safety measures were considered too costly. Little was known about industrial diseases, and still less done to prevent them.

Finally, there is unemployment insurance, which even now ranks among the less common forms of social insurance. This is surprising, since unemployment has been considered one of the major plagues of modern industrial society. Unemployment insurance is mentioned with specific approval in the social writings of the popes. It is particularly valuable for workers in industries subject to seasonal unemployment, since they will thus have assured income for the entire year. By contrast, many such insurance systems are of limited value when a long period of idleness occurs. Workers often run out of their benefit period and hence are reduced to public-assistance programmes.

In addition to the forms of social legislation considered above, there are several others which fall within the scope of the moral principles promulgated by the popes.

In the judgement of Pius XI and John XXIII, much of the credit for this trend should be given to the pioneer encyclical, *Rerum Novarum*. When we consider this in conjunction with the development in social thought of recent popes, it can truly be said that the Church is friend and protector to the workers of the world.

PART II

FROM THE INDUSTRIAL REVOLUTION TO THE PRESENT DAY

By

HARRY W. FLANNERY

CHAPTER VII

THE INDUSTRIAL

REVOLUTION

ENGLAND

The Industrial Revolution came to England first. From the dawn of history until the middle of the eighteenth century men made all their goods by hand. They had some simple tools, the wheel, the level, the crane and some elementary cutting tools, but that was all. Suddenly all was changed. One invention led to another: men who had to twist each thread separately by hand, now had a machine that twisted hundreds of threads at once, supervised by one man. The next thing was machinery weaving the thread into cloth. James Watt improved the steam engine and there was power to drive the new machinery. Richard Trevithick produced a pump for the deep mining of coal for the engines. George Stephenson invented the locomotive. Coal was rapidly moved to the factories, the finished goods to the ports, where steamboats gradually replaced sailing ships. The Luddites[1] set out at night to destroy the machines that were preventing their

[1] The "Luddite Rioters" or Luddites were organized bands of workmen who gave expression to the dismay of the workers at the introduction of machinery and the consequent scarcity in the demand for manual labour. They destroyed all kinds of machinery, particularly stocking and lace frames in the Midlands. The name is derived from Ned Ludd who destroyed a machine in a fit of temper in 1779. The Luddite riots lasted from 1811 to 1818. *Editor.*

getting work, but nothing could stop the new wave of progress.

The Industrial Revolution which had thus begun in England was to spread to the rest of the Western world. In England smoking factory chimneys were the signs of the new age of prosperity for management, merchants and shipowners. Production and profits boomed as never before. The towns and cities of England quadrupled their populations. Sheep raising took the place of farming and displaced farm workers were obliged to seek work in the cities. The Irish, in the grip of the famine caused by the failure of the potato crop (1845-7), flocked into England in search of food and work on any terms. Authorities in Ireland paid the passage for thousands of the hungry and the sick, with most of the ships crowded far beyond their capacities.

Most of the Irish were Catholics so that the result of this mass immigration was the doubling of the Catholic population in the industrial cities particularly in the North (Liverpool, Manchester, Leeds, for example) and elsewhere (Bristol and Birmingham) during the years 1841-51. They crowded into the very worst districts of the cities. South-east Lancashire was one of the blackest spots. It was said that nowhere else in the world was there an area so large with so high a density of population. The unskilled Irish, most of whom had previously worked on farms, had to take what they could get.

In the great industrial cities and elsewhere the housing conditions of the workers were deplorable. Streets were unpaved, unlit and there was no sewerage system. Few houses had a water supply. Many families were obliged to find refuge in damp cellars. Streets were cluttered with refuse and heaps of filth because of the lack of sanitary facilities. Under such conditions it is hardly surprising that intemperance was common among the Irish and other factory workers, and disease was prevalent.

Despite the efforts of social reformers like Lord Shaftesbury and others it cannot be denied that conditions were appalling. Private charity did what it could but it was a very small contribution in the face of an immense problem. Charity towards the poor was urged on the well-to-do and the poor themselves were exhorted to bear their lot in patience, to be resigned to their poverty after the example of our Lord. In the spirit of the times little more seemed necessary; the liberalism of the mercantile age, of *laissez-faire* individualism, held that economic life was regulated by its own natural laws, and should not be subject to interference by the State or any other group. The liberals of this period argued that business and industry must be left free and the greatest common good would result. This would come about, it was asserted, because in the struggle for survival men would produce to the best of their ability. The sum total, then, would be the maximum production of the highest quality possible, with the good of everyone served. But for this process to be successful, there must be no political or private interference. Competition must be left completely untrammelled. Furthermore, it was believed, business and industry had no responsibility for the poor, including their own employees, except, perhaps, through individual charity.

At the beginning of the Industrial Revolution the Catholic Church in England, after upwards of two centuries of persecution and proscription, was possibly at the lowest ebb in its fortunes. The majority of Catholics were poor and the clergy not numerous. Some of the more important families which had kept the faith became increasingly impoverished. The influx of Irish at the time of the famine and afterwards coincided with the beginning of the turn of the tide, in the 'forties of the nineteenth century, when the wave of converts, largely the result of the Oxford Movement, brought new life to what, in 1829, the year of Catholic Emancipation, was almost a moribund community of some 200,000. With the converts (John Henry Newman standing head and shoulders above them all) the large numbers of Irish immigrants were to infuse new life into the Church in England, but not for a generation or so. In the 'forties their presence created a problem for the Church rather than an asset.

In the circumstances it is hardly surprising that the problem was not adequately faced: the shortage of priests and the prevailing social conscience of the period (naturally enough shared by the English Catholics) both combined to make the plight of the Irish workers sorry indeed. It must be said, however, that numbers of priests worked heroically among the Irish in the North of England, some giving their lives while ministering to their flocks during the frequent epidemics.

Normal government was restored to the Church in England when Cardinal Nicholas Wiseman was made archbishop of Westminster at the head of a province composed of twelve diocesan sees. This was in 1850.[2] Although by this time the Catholic population had grown to something like 679,000, the problems of the growing Church, the provision of Catholic primary schools, the building of churches, training of the clergy, in a word the re-establishment of the Church in England, left little energy or resources for social work or the formation of an enlightened social conscience ahead of that of the country at large. Yet right at the outset, in his "Appeal to the Reason and Good Feeling on the Subject of the Catholic Hierarchy" Cardinal Wiseman made it clear where the mission of the newly appointed hierarchy principally lay. He had been accused of laying claim to the material and historical treasures of Westminster Abbey: "This splendid monument," he wrote,

> its treasures of art and its fitting endowments, form not the part of Westminster which will concern me. . . . Close to the Abbey of Westminster there lie concealed labyrinths of lanes and courts and alleys and slums—nests of ignorance, vice, depravity and crime, as well as squalor, wretchedness

[2] For a full account of the history of the Church in the British Isles during the nineteenth century see M. P. Carthy, O.S.U. *Catholicism in English-speaking Lands,* volume 92 in this series (volume 91 in the English edn).

and disease. . . . This is the part of Westminster which alone I could and which alone I shall be glad to claim and to visit as a blessed pasture in which sheep of holy Church are to be tended, in which a bishop's godly work has to be done.

Wiseman's voice thus early spoke out for the poor, but it was left to his successor, Henry Edward Manning, to add justice to charity in urging the cause of the poor, the worker and his family. He emphasized the responsibilities of individuals, of society and the State, and insisted that the workers had rights. His appearance at the Exeter Hall in London (December, 1872) on behalf of the Agricultural Labourer's Union showed clearly where his sympathies lay in the conflict between masters and workmen. Writing, subsequently, to Gladstone, at that time Prime Minister, he said:

> As to the agricultural affair . . . why cannot you . . . prohibit the labour of children under a certain age? Compel payment of wages in money. Regulate the number of dwellings according to the population of the parishes. Establish tribunals of arbitration in counties for questions between labour and land.

One of Manning's most memorable pronouncements came in 1875 in a speech to the Leeds Mechanics Institute on "The Dignity and Rights of Labour." He declared that labour, rather than capital or even skill, was the cause of wealth and the origin of England's greatness. He defined labour as "the honest exertion of the powers of mind and body for our own good and the good of our neighbour. . . . Any man who fulfils the lot of his existence is in a state of dignity." Manning continued:

> I claim for labour the rights of property. . . . The working man carries his property with him as ready money. He can buy with it, and he can sell it. He can exchange it. He can set a price on it. Labour has a right not only to its own freedom, but it has a right to protect itself. . . . The homes of the poor in London are often very miserable. The state of the houses—families living in single rooms, sometimes many families in one room, a corner apiece. These things cannot go on; these things ought not to go on. The accumulation

of wealth like mountains, in the possession of classes and of individuals, cannot go on. These moral conditions of our people must be healed. No Commonwealth can rest on such foundations.

Manning asserted that the worker had the right to determine for whom he should work and at what wages. He said that he could conceive of nothing more entirely in accord with natural rights and with the highest jurisprudence than that those who had a common interest should unite for the promotion of that interest. To Manning, the right of association was incontestable. He said it might be local as in townships, accidental and ephemeral as in meetings for discussion or action, or limited and restricted, as in unions of workers. And he did not hesitate to recognize in principle the legitimacy of the strike, as frequently the only weapon in the hands of the workers in the face of the despotism of capital.

If association failed, Manning continued, it was necessary to have recourse to the State. Further, when the State intervenes, it ought to be on the side of the weaker, for there is no equality of struggle between the worker and his employer. The Cardinal stated the further basic principle that work is not a commodity, a value regulated by economic laws, but a human and social act, with moral consequences for the worker and his family. As had happened to those who argued for the workingman, Manning was called a "socialist". His intervention to protect women and children in their hours and conditions of work and to restrict night and Sunday work met with few serious objections. On the other hand, his arguments for trade union organization, limitation of the hours of labour, and for the establishment of a minimum wage were the subject of brisk controversy.

In 1880 in a Lenten pastoral, Manning contrasted the great wealth of England, created by the acceleration of industrial and commercial activity, with the continuing very great poverty. In 1885 in the *Dublin Review,* he called for a change in the land laws of England. He pointed to the great amount of land in England that was in the hands of a few landlords; the "have-nots" and the "lack lands", he feared, were ripe for revolution.

When an unemployment crisis occurred in England in 1885, the English Catholic leader denounced *The Times* for being "heartless and heedless" for advocating that those who were employed produce as much profit as possible so that employers would have enough money to engage more labour. Manning's statement at this time that "every man has a right to work or to bread" was denounced as socialist and dangerous.

An industrial depression began in the 'seventies and London became uncomfortably familiar with processions of the workless. Violence occasionally resulted when tempers flared. The continued unrest was worrying the Cardinal, and he sought a means to end it. "The only practical scheme would be in the apportionment of wages to the employers' profit, subject to periodical revision. Sliding scales and bonuses are sure to get out of gear," he wrote to Sir Samuel Boulton. The refusal of the employers to open their books "implied to me fear and suspicion, something to hide—that is, disproportioned gains".

Manning fought for the improvement of the British Poor Laws, supported the Shop Hours League in its campaign to close shops earlier on one day a week, was a patron of the Co-operative Clothing Company, subscribed to the Stead Defence Fund for the protection of young girls, joined forces with Cardinal Gibbons of the United States when the Knights of Labor there seemed in danger of being proscribed by Rome, and won acclaim for intervention in the Dockers' Strike of 1889, when he succeeded in bringing about a settlement in the dockers' favour. Of the dock strike he wrote, "It is not true that such contests are the private affairs of masters and men. But this theory will not die until it is killed by public catastrophe."

When Leo XIII's historic encyclical *Rerum Novarum* was

published, Manning cried out, "The Holy Father has taken the millions who labour under his protection. So must the bishops of England. God forbid that we should be looked upon as the servants of plutocracy, instead of the guides and guardians of the poor." Leo was impressed by Manning as much, if not more, than by any other churchman who was then pointing the way that, with the arrival of the industrial age, must be followed if the worker was not to be oppressed, but be given all he and his family must have in justice and charity. Both Leo in Rome and Manning in London had much in common. They were both aristocrats by birth and training, and for many years had been distressed by the plight of the poor. Each spoke out loud and clear on the challenge that Catholics and non-Catholics, theologians and lawyers, educators and legislators, as well as management and labour must inescapably accept as a moral responsibility.

GERMANY

Today there are two Germanys; at the beginning of the eighteenth century there were three: Prussia, Austria, and the Reich Estates, the last divided between the Protestant and Catholic territories. The Holy Roman Empire of the German Nation was breaking up, finally coming to an end in 1806. As the authority of the empire faded, the bishops and ecclesiastical estates acquired unlimited secular authority over their territories, principally Cologne, Trier and Mainz. These ecclesiastical territories became a sort of absolutist Church-State, strong enough to function independently.

Eighteenth-century Catholicism in the ecclesiastical territories demonstrated neither political nor social responsibility despite dire poverty, political illiteracy and social backwardness. In addition, since the ecclesiastical princes were antagonistic to the Protestant States, they shut their areas off from progress, particularly in the economic sphere. L. Haeusser, in his *Deutsche Geschichte vom Tode Friedrichs des Grossen bis zur Gründung des Deutschen Bundes,* said that at this time,

> Distress and extreme need were rarely in evidence, but there was great poverty. The ecclesiastical territories were a paradise for contemplative spiritual inaction and highly aristocratic idleness. . . . While everywhere efforts were directed to putting available resources to the best possible use, thereby improving agriculture, industry, and commerce, here the rich produce of the land provided an income to be spent on pleasures, partly outside of the country, and thus withdrawn uselessly from the working population. Statecraft of this sort did not bring about gradually rising standards for a thrifty, laborious, well-to-do population. It did result in feeding fifty clerics and 260 beggars for each one thousand inhabitants on every square mile of these ecclesiastical territories.

Germany, at this time, was almost completely agricultural. Only a quarter of the population lived in towns, including those places dignified by the name, even though less than two thousand persons lived in them. There was weaving in Silesia, cutlery making in Solingen, and production of clocks and toys in the Black Forest, but peasants did the work in their homes.

Napoleon ended the Holy Roman Empire of the German Nation. With the occupation of the Rhineland in 1793, ecclesiastical rule in the territories on the left bank came to an end, particularly in the electorates of Cologne, Trier and Mainz. The Act of Secularization in 1803 gave the secular governments the further right of acquiring all ecclesiastical sovereignties, institutions and properties on the right bank as reparation for their losses left of the Rhine. Final dissolution of the Empire came in the Paris Treaty of 1806, as a result of which Francis II, of the Holy Roman Empire, became Francis I of Austria. The way was set for a new federalized Germany.

"The separation [of Church and State] has caused the emancipation of religion and its resurrection from the dust," commented Franz von Baader, the first important Catholic social voice in Germany, called "the spiritual father of the Christian Social movement in Germany". Baader, born in Munich in 1765, a physician by profession, practised for thirty years as a mining engineer, and while in England, 1792 to 1796, he became concerned about the plight of the worker in the new industrial society. He devoted himself to the study of Augustine, Anselm of Canterbury and Thomas Aquinas and set down the principles of a modern Catholic sociology.

This German social pioneer of the industrial age rejected Adam Smith and the principle of *laissez faire*. This he said is "loose talk." Its application causes the worker to exchange "land servitude . . . for the even harsher and more oppressive money servitude." In the present state of affairs, he argued, the power is all in the hands of the wage masters. The answer is not "in the foolish conclusions that it would be best to put an end to this progress of industry and mechanization; we should, on the contrary, become wise by experience so that we may learn to avoid the cliffs which the States we mentioned [France and England] were unable to avoid." Needed, he declared, are acceptance of basic Christian principles and the association of workers "against their wage masters," with State protection for the associations.

Among the principles set down by Baader were these:

Christianity does admit of the power of men over men, but it does not admit of one man being in the power of another, as his chattel.

Every use and consumption of property that is not social is anti-social. For he who does not live for society lives against it. . . . No Christian may declare: this property, this right, this office are mine, to handle as I please; for in reality, these are God's gifts and tasks, and a Christian may handle them only as it pleases God. . . . Since according to Christ's teachings men, be they the highest or humblest, exist only by the grace of God, by that same token they cannot and must not do and deal with their persons, their powers and their property as in their own selfish way they like, but only as God wills.

Baader and French Abbé Félicité de Lamennais conferred together in Munich in 1832 and agreed that the mediating services of a socially-minded priesthood were needed. Lamennais in his Munich article called for a social office "of the priest who should stand as a disinterested third party between the two parties who form the compact, to serve as a common bond between the rich who provide the money and the soil and the poor who can only contribute work to the common fund." Baader conceived of the rôle of the priest as "an advocate and aid in the plight of the property-less among the people, and as an arbiter between them and the property owners."

The workers, he insisted, had the right to join together in associations, protected by the State. They are entitled "to be represented by an advocate and this right must be guaranteed them unconditionally in our modern constitutionally governed States. This representation must be administered through spokesmen elected by themselves who, however, should not be assisted by counsel who are public servants or civil servants of any kind, nor lawyers in the strict sense, but should be priests whom they can completely trust."

Baader demanded the kind of social deaconry of priests that found its expression in the years to come in his own country of Germany through Ketteler, Kolping, Hitze, and other informed and dedicated clergymen everywhere.

Wilhelm Emmanuel von Ketteler, called "the most outstanding social, political and spiritual leader in 19th century German Catholicism," first won national attention in Germany's potentially historic year, 1848. It was in May of that year that South German leaders summoned the German Constituent Assembly to the *Paulskirche* in Frankfurt. Ketteler was sent to this first national parliament of Germany by the voters of Tecklenburg, Westphalia, as one of those aspiring young men, chosen by universal manhood suffrage, who hoped to bring democracy to their country. It was a gallant gathering, high among constitutional conventions, but one hundred years before its time.

The national assembly failed, but twenty-three of the Catholic leaders in Frankfurt met with twelve others in the First General Conference of Catholics on October 4th, in Mainz. This group eventually became Germany's Centre and later Christian Democratic Party, with its ranks widened, on the urging of Ketteler and others, to include non-Catholics. The two main speakers in Mainz were Ketteler and Ritter von Buss, the first German to propose a bill of social reforms in any German parliament.

Among other things, Buss asserted that, "The journeymen must again sit at table together with their masters so that they will not feel slighted and consequently become merged with a rabble of proletarians." Buss advocated technical training for workers and proposed that the State set up a system of savings accounts through which workers might eventually own their own factories. The State, he said, should insure the workers so that in time of sickness they would not have to draw upon their private savings. These accounts, Buss declared, should be made up from weekly deductions from wages, matched by the State with an equal contribution. Buss also asked for a statutory limitation of fourteen working hours a day, and with no work on Sundays.

Germany, at the time, was just coming into the industrial age. Industrial development began in Germany a century later than in England, but the people along the Rhine covered in a few decades what had transpired more gradually across the Channel. The failure of farm crops in 1846 and 1847 hastened the process, as dispossessed farmers flocked to the cities in search of work, and small owners sold their land to go into the factories. With an excess of workers over jobs, industrialists cut wages drastically. Children, as well as adults, worked exhausting hours for meagre pay.

Ketteler was educated at Göttingen, Heidelberg, Munich, and Berlin. He was a Prussian civil servant until the time when, in 1837, he broke with the government over a demand of the State that the children of mixed marriages follow the faith of the father. From Berlin, Ketteler went to Munich, where he joined a group of young Catholic intellectuals, studied theology and canon law, taught law at the University of Munich and decided to devote his life to the Church, being ordained on June 1st, 1844, at the age of thirty-three. After Beckum, Hopsten and St Hedwig's in Berlin, Ketteler was, just five years later, in 1849, bishop of Mainz.

On September 21st, 1848, Ketteler preached the funeral oration in Frankfurt for two conservative deputies killed in a street riot. The solution of the social question, Ketteler declared, does not lie in men taking the law into their own hands. Germany, asserted Ketteler, needed social reform, something that had not even been mentioned in the *Paulskirche* debates. We can "realize the aims and aspirations of the workers only in the closest union with religion and with Christ. It is the only true hope." The Mainz sermons on "The Great Social Question of Our Time" were the first appeals to the Germans to take up their social deaconry. They were the real foundation of German Catholicism's social movement, although like so many other pronouncements, they were called "socialistic-communistic preachments," and much of what Ketteler said was unheeded.

Adolph Kolping (1813-65), who set up the *Katholische Gesellenvereine,* the Catholic Journeymen's Association in 1851, was an associate and friend of Ketteler. Due to Ketteler's support, a Kolping branch was opened in Mainz, and youth organizations for the care of apprentices were also set up in Darmstadt, Bingen, Offenbach and Bensheim. Ketteler sought to do what he could to help young Catholic workers as they travelled in the exercise of their crafts. Ketteler called upon every bishop in Germany to build, buy or rent a house for the *Gesellenvereine,* which he also urged be opened to other than Catholic workers.

Although he promoted the formation of workers' associations, Ketteler did not believe that the Church should form labour unions or direct them, but he urged State protection of such associations. At the same time, Christianity should "hasten to the aid of the workers and bring into reality in ever widening circles the idea of the production association. The goal of all social programmes, as Ketteler saw it, was more than seeing that workers got higher wages. He also advocated a bonus, saying that at the end of the year when wages and other expenses have been taken care of, profits should be divided with the employees sharing in them. Payment would be made half in cash and the other half would be turned back into company funds, but credited to the workers, as shares. All workers must belong to such organizations, according to his craft, business or industry, said Ketteler.

Ferdinand Lassalle (1825-1864) had been a disciple of Karl Marx but broke with him in 1862 and became the founder of German Social Democracy and of the German Workers' Alliance in 1863. Lassalle was a hero among the workers, and his picture hung on the walls of many worker homes alongside the crucifix. Lassalle was often in controversy with Ketteler, but they shared basic agreements. At one time, Lassalle, in his *Arbeiterprogramm* (Workers' Programme), called the workers, "the rock upon which the Church of the present ought to be built". Although some Catholic priests had forbidden workers to join the General German Workers' Alliance, and had even refused members absolution, Ketteler on May 25th, 1866, declared that "generally speaking, I find that the original goals of the General German Workers' Alliance in so far as I know them and in so far as they have been publicly announced, are compatible with goals that a Catholic of good standing might hold." At the same time, Ketteler reminded the workers that the promises made by the socialists must be given a Christian foundation. "Without religion and without morality," he repeated, "all efforts to better the condition of the worker will be without success."

Ketteler, who was originally against legislation to protect the interests of the worker, later insisted that "the State must protect workers against exploitation, fraud, mistreatment and tyranny". The same notes maintained that the State should also prohibit the work of women in factories, in the interests "of family life, with each man a wife and each child a mother." Work of children of school age should also be prohibited. Sunday rest must be required. Ketteler described the poverty of the workers in "The Labour Question and Christianity," saying at one point:

> The great masses of the people who belong to the dispossessed have been brought into such condition of want, even for the most essential things, that their plight may not only be said to be inhuman, but it may be said that it is such that it will lead, with necessity, to the most terrible struggle within our society in a battle between the rich and the poor just as history has recorded what took place in ancient society.

The State in this situation, said the German social leader, has not only the right, but the duty to interfere.

Ketteler recommended the strike when necessary, pointing out that it had been the chief weapon of the English trade unions in effecting pay increases that had ranged from thirteen to fifty per cent. He warned at the same time against excessive demands.

Ketteler was a member of the Reichstag in 1871, but he resigned after a short period of service, saying that it was no place for a Catholic bishop. Afterwards, he worked with others in founding the Centre Party, so named because it was set up to form a balance between the Conservatives and the Progressives. Ketteler himself wanted to invite Protestants as well as Catholics into the party. "The difference which separates us Catholics from you Protestants must be forgotten," he wrote. "We must all stand together against the unbelief which threatens all justice and morality, all who believe in Christ and a living God and a hope for eternal happiness."

Clemens von Galen, nephew of Ketteler, introduced the Ketteler resolutions in the Reichstag, calling for prohibition of hiring of youths under fourteen in any factory, protection of family life through limitation of women in factories, industrial courts of arbitration with freely elected representation for the workers, restriction of Sunday work to essential public services, old-age insurance, and other provisions for worker protection. Each of these proposals was eventually enacted.

Leo XIII, whose *Rerum Novarum* lighted the way for social justice all over the world, called Ketteler his great predecessor (*mon grand précurseur*), and in a private audience with the bishop's last secretary said on August 30th, 1896: "Ketteler was a great bishop. He was the first to openly state the responsibility and duty of capital and the State to the working men of our times." A comparison of *Rerum Novarum* and the speeches and writings of Ketteler shows a close resemblance not only in content, but in the very order of their appearance. Leo, of course, drew from many great churchmen of his time as well as from his own personal observations, but one of the chief advisers who did the research work for the first great labour encyclical was Karl Emil von Vogelsang, an admirer of the teachings of Ketteler, about which he wrote in his paper, *Das Vaterland*. Vogelsang was a convert to Catholicism under the influence of Ketteler and the Munich circle of Görres, at Innsbruck in 1850.

Franz Hitze (1851-1921), Westphalian workmen's priest, was the most important among those who carried on Ketteler's ideas after the bishop's death at the age of sixty-six (July 13th, 1877). Hitze stepped into the controversy about Catholic labour unions, more or less initiated by Ketteler's promotion of the idea of "associations". The Social-Romanticist group around Görres promoted confessional unions under clerical leadership and clerical politics. This effort was largely centred in publications in Munich and Mainz, and Franz Hitze during his student years in Würzburg and Rome was among those influenced. In an essay in 1880, Hitze stated the thinking at the time of himself and his compatriots: "We demand a corporate order of society instead of the Socialist people's State with its lack of structure; we demand corporative liberty and equality, both legally as against the reactionary attempts of the Junkers and factually as against the wage slavery under liberal capitalism."

Meanwhile the Christan Social and Catholic labour associations that had developed under Ketteler's initiative had a membership of only 20,000, while the Socialist organizations were flourishing. Hitze came from Rome to the industrial town of München-Gladbach, saw "with his own eyes the widespread distress, the hardships and injustice of the social conditions," and he was no longer interested so much in idealism as in the most immediate and effective means of improving the conditions of the workers.

The idealist turned realist worked for his objectives from 1898 to 1912 as a member of the Prussian Diet, and from 1884 to 1921 as a member of the Reichstag. He was a modest, hard-working legislator, not often taking part in the public debates, but working faithfully through personal contacts and in the committees. Hitze presented social justice as a principle to which all men of good will should subscribe.

The German labour education movement, which has since developed into one of the best in the world, also began under Hitze. *Arbeiterwohl* (workers' welfare) was founded in 1881, with Hitze executive secretary and editor of the association's publication. Then came the Christian Social Workmen's Associations, which formed the nucleus for the *Gewerkvereine,* trade associations, organized after 1894.

Through the patient, practical and far-seeing work of men like Baader, Ketteler, and others, all German workers and their families benefited.

FRANCE

The worker was the forgotten man in the first years of the French Revolution which exploded with the march on the Bastille and almost simultaneously in the nation's mines and mills. The years of France's political transformation from the *Ancien Régime* to the Third Republic, through the throes of the Revolution, the Constituent Assembly, the Legislative Assembly, the Reign of Terror, the exploits of Napoleon Bonaparte, and all the phases of a consulate, monarchy, and empire, formed the era of economic liberalism. Voices were raised in the cause of the worker, but while the owners of the factories and mines were amassing wealth, the workers and their families starved. Little was done for them in these decades.

Catholic social writing, speaking, and action during this period was considerable, but not very effective. The Revolution's Declaration of the Rights of Man was more concerned with liberty than with equality. The Charter of 1815, in the spirit of *laissez faire,* made property inviolable and prohibited associations of workmen. Most of the legislators stood staunch for freedom of every kind, and resolved that there should be no interference in operation of what they considered the inviolate law of supply and demand.

Meanwhile, in the textile mills of Alsace in 1828, the normal working day was fourteen or fifteen hours. At Mulhouse, work began generally at five o'clock in the morning and continued to eight or nine at night. In some factories the working day was as long as seventeen hours, with a half hour for lunch and an hour for dinner. At Lille, four-year-old children toiled in the shops. The average wage for an adult man was two francs (forty cents), one franc for a woman, seventy-five centimes for a child between thirteen and sixteen, and forty-five centimes (fifteen cents) for a child between eight and twelve years of age. One investigator reported in 1847 that workers were employed twenty-four hours a day in northern France. Real wages were lower in the eighteenth century than at the end of the fifteenth. Instead of benefiting the worker, the Industrial Revolution made his condition worse than it had ever been under feudalism or even slavery.

The Baron de Morogues estimated that in 1832 an industrial worker might be able to earn at one and a half francs a day, about 450 francs a year. The cost of supporting his family (figuring three children, which was normal) would be conservatively 860 francs, without providing for sickness, accident, or saving. Since a workman could not earn much more than half what he needed for existence, his wife and children also worked. In such a case, a family could barely subsist, barring illness, accidents, or industrial troubles, which were frequent. In such a case, workers' families became destitute paupers and sometimes criminals.

Employment of children was justified by those who pointed out that their small fingers were more delicate and dextrous, that they were better able to mend threads, that they had a suppleness of body and could more easily glide under the looms. Further, it was said, it was good to keep the family together during the working day. And, in addition, child labour, being cheaper, was necessary to meet competition. Many children became dwarfed or deformed.

One of the outstanding first Catholic spokesmen for the workers was Abbé Félicité de Lamennais (1782-1854). With his associates, he founded *L'Avenir* (October 16th, 1830), which proclaimed on its masthead: "God and Liberty."

One of Lamennais' associates was Jean-Baptiste-Henri-Dominique Lacordaire, who argued (1848) in a magnificent *sorites:*

> Between the strong and the weak, between the rich and the poor, between the master and the servant, it is liberty which oppresses and law which makes man free. . . . *Laissez faire* is the abandonment of the weak to the hands of the strong. . . . Whenever laws have been made they have been for the protection of the weakest. . . . The workingman is weaker than the master. . . . Therefore, the worker should be protected by law.

Lamennais himself demanded liberation of the Church from the control of the State, a full franchise for the people, and their protection from the State through freedom of the press, education, association and assembly. He said workers must be protected against exploitation and have the right to organize. Lamennais led the first Christian Democratic movement in French history, according to Joseph N. Moody.

Charles de Coux, Catholic professor whose studies in political economy led him to put high hopes in Catholic social principles, was also with *L'Avenir*. "Catholicism," he wrote, "in its practical consequences, presents the most admirable system of social economy that has ever been given to the world. . . . Today the combat is essentially the same as in the Middle Ages; Catholicism is now at grips with the aristocracy of capital as formerly with the aristocracy of the land."

The editors of *L'Avenir* were provocative and aroused Louis Philippe's government (1830-48), bishops who did not wish to forgo the certainty of State payment of their salaries for the doubtful generosity of their flocks, and even leaders in provincial capitals who feared what might happen next in France. At the same time, the popularity of the paper among the young clergy and seminarians did not help Lamennais' cause.

Pressure was exerted upon Rome by French, English and Austrian members of the hierarchy to stop the publication of *L'Avenir*. Pius VIII paid little attention, but his successor, Gregory XVI, felt obliged to act when Lamennais, beleaguered on all sides, went to the Vatican to plead his case. The pope listened and gave his answer in the encyclical *Mirari Vos*. Although *L'Avenir* was not mentioned, the major tenets advanced in the paper were denounced. Lamennais himself was so deeply distressed that he left the Church. He tried to continue to write, but no longer had the fire of his former brilliance. De Coux, on the other hand, who wrote the leading economic articles for the journal, continued his activities through other publications and politics.

Through the Vicomte de Villeneuve-Bargemont (1784-1850), Catholic deputy and economist, de Coux won the first victory against the government's stand to prevent legislative interference in labour-management relations. De Coux and Villeneuve-Bargemont were primarily concerned about the treatment of children in factories and urged the Chamber of Deputies to set a maximum working day of eight hours for children under eight years of age; in 1841 Villeneuve-Bargemont succeeded in getting the legislation passed. Charles de Montalembert, who had collaborated with Lacordaire and Lamennais, successfully carried on the fight for the same law in the House of Peers. Their victory was the first by Catholic social pioneers against the conscienceless classical Liberal economists. Villeneuve-Bargemont and Montalembert were aided in their efforts by the agitation, outside the legislature, of people like Cardinal Croy, Archbishop of Rouen, and the Vicomte Armand de Melun.

Villeneuve-Bargemont (1784-1850) was the leading legislative influence of the period. He had been an administrative official under the Empire (1804-1812), a prefect, councillor of State in 1828, and in 1830 was elected to the national legislature. He first became interested in social legislation after a visit to Lille, with its 32,000 paupers out of a population of 70,000. After that experience, he called for legislative intervention to help relieve some of the worst situations, and, beyond that, systematic regulation.

> If one looks for the numerous causes of this general and perpetual poverty, one is compelled to recognize that the first and most active of all is found in the principle of an almost unlimited production and of an equally unlimited competition, which imposes upon industrial *entrepreneurs* the ever-growing obligation of lowering the price of labour, and upon the workingmen the necessity of surrendering themselves, their wives and their children to a labour the excessive quantity and duration of which exceed the measure of their strength, and for a wage which does not always suffice for the most wretched existence.

In other words, the trouble was with the system, not with industrialists and machines, but with those who supported a principle that treated people like machines. Villeneuve-Bargemont saw the situation as "the great problem of our age". He advocated that social balance between the power of the manufacturers and workers be attained through organization of the latter; that manufacturers employing more than fifty workers be obliged by law to maintain healthful shop conditions, with such conditions assured through regular inspections; that such manufacturers establish schools for adult workers, refuse employment to anyone who is under fourteen years of age and has not received a medical certificate of fitness for industrial work, refuse employment to anyone who cannot read, write or do simple arithmetic; separate men and women workers, guarantee respect for religion and good morals, and set up workers' provident or insurance funds.

Villeneuve-Bargemont insisted that "a just rate of wages be the first condition of all industrial enterprise". The profit of the employer should be taken only after the worker had been paid an adequate wage. Such a wage, he explained, should enable the worker to obtain nourishing food, clean and durable clothes, a dwelling warm in winter and capable of ventilation in summer. The wage should be enough to properly support a wife and two children, with sufficient beyond that for sickness and old age. Said this man, one of the first economists to advocate a "living wage": "If the wage cannot provide all these things for the workingman, it is no longer in conformity with the laws not only of nature, of justice, and of charity, but even of political prudence."

Aware that industrial conditions in other countries like England and Germany affected France, Villeneuve-Bargemont called for international labour organization. He asked, "Could it not be established in principle, for example, that the daily duration of effective labour, for all workers, should not exceed thirteen hours, twelve hours, or any other limit deemed proper?"

Villeneuve-Bargemont, as a recognized economist, and as a man who had experience in administrative and legislative matters, and who had observed conditions in other countries as well as his own, was quoted even by the socialists as an authority.

Vicomte Armand de Melun (1807-77), who aided Villeneuve-Bargemont and Montalembert in their first successful break in the stand of the liberals of that day against legislative intervention on behalf of workers, carried on the battle. An aristocrat by birth, Melun decided after the July, 1830, revolution, to devote his life to social work. He began with the poor in the Quartier Saint-Médard, and organized several charitable organizations. Although he continued his charitable work, Melun devoted more and more time to seeking legislative remedies. He was first concerned with efforts to revive the old guilds and to restrict child labour. After the revolution of 1848, Melun entered parliament to fight for his objectives.

His ideas of social legislation were set out in a pamphlet, "The Intervention of Society to Prevent and Alleviate Poverty." He believed that in the first place preventive legislation was more desirable than remedial, that it was more reasonable to take steps to prevent the workingman from starving or becoming a pauper than to try to aid him when he and his family were tragic victims, and secondly, it is just as logical to protect the worker against ignorance, sickness, poverty, excessive labour, and unemployment, as against theft and murder, all of which affect his safety and happiness.

Melun and other Catholic deputies worked through a committee.

> Treated as a socialist by the majority with whom I vote [he commented at one time], as a philanthropic idiot by the great politicians, as an enemy of private and religious charity by the bishops and the Catholics, I am nevertheless held responsible by many for the inaction of the committee, which I convoke every day and which I urge forward with all my strength.

Melun's Committee of Thirty had some success. The Legislative Assembly of 1850 voted a law on insanitary dwellings, pension funds, and on the education and guardianship of juvenile offenders. The committee also presented bills on hospitals, medical service in the country, apprenticeship, employment of women and children in factories. However, the committee itself rejected many of Melun's proposals so that they never reached the floor of the assembly. In fact one of the committee reports called many of his ideas "chimerical and impracticable."

Melun commented that the report asserted "that it was necessary for poor humanity to live with its maladies, fearing lest it kill itself in attempting a curse." He declared that the poor would hardly benefit from "this voluminous masterpiece. . . . The most eloquent pages give very little warmth or nourishment to people who suffer from cold and hunger."

When Louis Napoleon's *coup d'état* occurred on December 2nd, 1851, Melun's political career came to an end. He was imprisoned for protesting.

Perhaps most noteworthy of all the fighters for Catholic social principles in this period was Frédéric Ozanam (1813-53), who first showed his interest when he was only eighteen years old: Saint-Simon's challenge to the pope to undertake a mission of social reform moved young Ozanam. He is remembered most today because he founded the Society of St Vincent de Paul, influenced Lacordaire to join with himself, Melun, de Coux and others in a new journal. They announced that the purpose of the publication was to reconcile religion and the democratic Republic, and as they demanded freedom of association and justice for workers, they called it *L'Ere Nouvelle* (The New Era), an organ of hope and confidence.

Hope and confidence were needed in 1848. A new legislature had just been elected, in which the Catholics were strong, but most of them came from country, rather than worker areas. The national assembly elected on April 23rd, 1848, included three Catholic bishops, ten priests and a number of Catholic laymen. The times were difficult. France was in a severe economic depression. Government loans were insecure. Banks were refusing to make payments. There was talk of nationalizing the railways. Unemployment grew. The workers of Paris, frustrated and miserable, "felt that they had made a revolution, only to be cheated of its fruits". On May 15th, a demonstration in favour of Poland flooded into the Palais Bourbon and threatened the newly elected assembly. Reaction was immediate. Montalembert called wasted his twenty years of attempts to translate Catholic social principles into social justice and order. Another Catholic deputy, Falloux, introduced a proposal to disband the National Workshops, public works projects, which provided some jobs for the jobless. The Chamber passed the bill on June 19th. The workers exploded in the June riots. Monsignor Affre, the archbishop of Paris, determined to halt the bloodshed, marched to the barricades, but was killed by a stray bullet. The workers repudiated the act, and the archbishop died with a plea for peace and mercy, but his death had the opposite effect from what he wished. The Catholic deputies were even more convinced of the impossibility of compromise. They joined in a conservative bloc as the Party of Order.

The workers, on the other hand, turned Left and became anticlerical. Karl Marx and Friedrich Engels published *The Communist Manifesto* in this year, 1848, and the Socialists came more and more under Marxian influence. Montalembert wrote in 1851, "to vote against Louis-Napoleon is to decide in favour of the Socialist revolution." As the Catholics supported the monarchy, the Socialists became even more anticlerical. Meanwhile, in this period, those Catholics who had been the major champions of Catholic social principles were moving from the scene. Villeneuve-Bargemont died in 1850. Melun, after 1851, devoted his time to social charity. Ozanam died in 1853, Lacordaire in 1861, de Coux in 1865.

Decades later, there was a resurgence of Catholic social thought, but it did not get to the ears of the workers. During this period, says Moody, the Church was even losing the peasants. Frederic Le Play, an engineer, and the Pretender, the Comte de Chambord, made proposals, but they looked upon the anachronistic monarchy as the means of attainment. Count Albert de Mun founded the Committee of Catholic Clubs, small in themselves, but the forerunner of the present Catholic social movement in France. Jacques Harmel and his son, Léon, formed guilds in their factories, but they were a form of paternalism, excellent in their way, but no answer to the pressing problems of the times.

Le Play was mistrustful of labour organization and opposed to legislation to correct the evils. Admitting that the moderate British factory Acts of 1833, 1842, 1844 and 1847, restricting the employment of women and children, had brought beneficial results, he nevertheless condemned government regulation of industry in principle.

Chambord, in his "Letter on Labour" (1865), spoke of "the necessity of voluntary and free association of workingmen for the defence of their common interests," but he showed himself fearful of such organizations, by saying that meetings must not be held without preliminary notice, and the government should have the right of representation at any meeting. At that time, labour unions still had no legal status in France. They were not permitted by law until 1884.

De Mun, a lieutenant with the ill-fated army of Metz, was taken prisoner by the Germans in the Franco-Prussian war in 1870. He was interned at Aix-la-Chapelle, where he learned of Bishop Ketteler's social justice programmes in Germany, and read what another writer had to say in a treatise on Catholicism and Democracy—Emile Keller, Catholic deputy from Belfort. Back from the war, de Mun went with a friend to a meeting of a small Catholic club of young workingmen on the Boulevard Montparnasse, in Paris. De Mun himself addressed the next meeting and convinced himself by his own oratory that he must form more such clubs. By 1884, de Mun and his associates had organized 400 committees and had 50,000 members in all parts of France.

Meanwhile, in 1876, de Mun sought election to the Chamber of Deputies and, though twice challenged and ousted, was reelected. In 1874, he took part in passing through the assembly another bill on child labour, this one excluding from "industrial labour in manufactories, mills,

mines, and workshops" all children under twelve, restricting
the hours of work to twelve hours a day for youngsters between the age of twelve to sixteen; prohibiting employment
of children at night, or on Sundays and legal holidays.

In 1880, Keller proposed a maximum working week of
sixty-one hours, instead of the seventy proposed by the
Chamber's committee; that the legislation apply to mines as
well as factories and mills; that employment of women at
night and in the first months of child-birth be prohibited.
The fight ended in establishing a six-day week with sixty-
six hours maximum.

De Mun argued for the right of workers to organize, but
he proposed that the guild form be revived with employers
sitting in the same association "united by the bond of Christian confraternity and common interests, in order to remedy
the antagonism which divided them, the isolation which
leaves the workers without protection against the abuses of
competition which leads to the decadence of the trade."

Under the present system, he said, "wages shrink, pauper-
ism spreads like a hideous leprosy, the exploited worker
feels the ferment of an implacable hatred growing in his
heart, and he has no recourse but to resistance and recourse
to war."

Between 1884 and 1889 de Mun made various proposals
for social reform and the improvement of working conditions,
and some of these were enacted in time: restriction of female
and child labour in 1892, 1900 and 1902; accident compensation in 1898; old-age assistance, 1905; old-age pensions,
1910; Sunday holidays, 1906.

With the death of Pius IX in 1878 and the accession of
Leo XIII a change of papal policy occurred. Leo XIII urged
French Catholics to come to terms with the Republic; un-
fortunately his appeal largely fell on deaf ears. With the
appearance of *Rerum Novarum,* however, some few of the
clergy and laity, among them de Mun, finally abandoned
their monarchist sentiments. Some of the younger clergy saw
clearly that the Church must accept political democracy and

promote social reforms. In 1896 a first national congress of a movement for social reform was held but, despite papal approval, by the turn of the century the effort had all but collapsed and with it any hope at the time of regaining the workers who had been lost to the Church.

THE UNITED STATES

Catholics in the United States, at the end of the American Revolution, numbered less than 25,000; the majority of them were farmers and planters, though there were some merchants and mechanics in the cities, such as Philadelphia. The Catholic population in the new country remained small in number until famine and pestilence occurred in Ireland and the 1848 democratic renaissance failed in Germany. By 1840, well over a half a million Catholics had arrived. The number exceeded three million during the next two decades, and by 1900, close to five million immigrants, largely Irish and Catholic, had crossed the ocean to the promised land. For the most part the newcomers were penniless, desperate, uneducated and bewildered. From Ireland, they came fresh from a contest with the landlord and the land agent, lured by stories of a land of freedom and opportunity for every man of native ability, energy and character. They came from farms and settled in the crowded, disorderly and insanitary cities, the ugly, dirty settlements near the coal fields, and the shacks that followed the westward trailing railroads. They came without skills or talents. Germans, fleeing from political disappointment, crowded into wretched tenements, though some went West to the freedom of open spaces. Then came the Italians and Slavs, before the United States closed its golden door against the "huddled masses yearning to breathe free, the wretched refuse of your teeming shores".

United States need of domestic manufacture did not begin until the new nation was cut off from England after the War of 1812, and the first industries, as almost everywhere in industrializing countries, were textile mills. Women and children did most of the work; in fact, this was believed to be the best arrangement, since the men thus did not have to be taken from the fields. At Lowell and other places in New England, factory boarding houses were set up, for the convenience and the protection of young New England farmers' daughters, who made up many of the first workers. The system was considered such a model, that Charles Dickens, after his 1842 American tour, recommended it to his English fellowmen.

Conditions changed since young girls stayed on the job only long enough to save enough to get married, with the result that mill owners hired more children and sought other workers wherever they could find them. As competition increased, wages were reduced and workers who had taken care of two looms were forced to handle four. Hours were "from sunrise to sundown," with public opinion assuming that the factory worker should labour no more and no less than the farmer, the shopkeeper and housewife.

As industry progressed and the number of immigrants increased, slum areas grew in Philadelphia, New York and Boston. Generally speaking, craftsmen were able to get better wages because they possessed needed skills, but all workers were the victims of recurrent depressions, known then as panics, and the fact that unions were illegal. An 1806 case involving eight shoemakers in Philadelphia was reported as a "combination and conspiracy to raise wages", and the jury came back with the verdict: "We find the defendants guilty of a combination to raise their wages."

The plight of the workers in America was a challenge to Catholic leadership, especially since most of the men and women in the mills and shops were Catholic. The situation was urgent since the religious world of the immigrants had been shattered. Most of them had been close to their church and their pastors in the old countries. Their religion had been a part with their work and their leisure, but they were now cast adrift in the troubled, new and predominantly Protestant land where their religion encountered considerable opposition.

One of the first Catholic laymen who arose in defence of the workers, especially the women, was Mathew Carey, publisher and philanthropist of Philadelphia, who arrived in the United States in 1784. Fr Augustus T. Thébaud, pastor of St Joseph's Church, Troy, New York, from 1852 to 1860, reported that American industry saw the relations between employers and employees as "strictly a matter of business, of wages and work."

Two converts to Catholicism were among the most able champions of the worker at this time: the philosopher-publicist, Orestes A. Brownson (1803-76) and the missionary priest, Isaac T. Hecker (1819-88). They were close friends and entered the Church in the same year, 1844. Both men believed that the Catholic Church had within its own teachings the answer to the social evils of the times. Brownson said many times that, when he entered the Church, his interest in the workingman was merely baptized. "I abandoned, indeed, after a year's devotion to it, the Workingmen's Party, but not the workingman's cause, and to that cause I have been faithful according to my light and ability," he said. Fr Hecker made one of the most important contributions to Catholic thinking about social matters when he began publication of the monthly *Catholic World* in 1865. Fr Hecker and his fellow Paulists were also active in war against social evils, especially intemperance and the saloon-keepers themselves.

German Catholics set up the German Catholic Central Verein in Baltimore, in April, 1855. The Central Verein sought to bring the social teachings of German Bishop Ketteler to the United States, and did much themselves in the field of sickness and life insurance, immigrant aid and employment.

In the midst of all this striving to aid the American worker, one of the most dramatic and tragic episodes of these days occurred in the anthracite coal fields of northeastern Pennsylvania. To these fields went immigrants, mostly Irish, from the 1840's to 1888. Mining was a hazardous occupation both for operators and miners. The operators had to invest huge sums, an estimated average being $100,000 for a colliery in 1873, and there were all sorts of risks inherent in the undertaking. Workers were in continuous danger of losing their health, their lives and their limbs. In Schuylkill, one of the six counties in the area, 566 miners were killed and 1,665 maimed in seven years; in 1871 alone, 112 were killed and 339 permanently injured. In a report to the governor of Pennsylvania, in 1875, P. F. M'Andrew wrote of the bad ventilation, the unreckoned misery of widows and orphans.

Wages were miserably low, and housing in many cases was indescribably bad. In 1839, a miner received a dollar a day, a labourer in the mines about eighty-two cents. Ten years later, the miner made a quarter more, the labourer a few cents more. Wages were reduced ten per cent or more since the miners had to buy everything from a postage stamp to a coffin from company stores, and, in addition, had to pay for their own blasting powder and tools. Since miners paid rent for their houses, some of them bare of furniture, men sometimes worked for a month in the mines and received, instead of wages, a statement cancelling their earnings completely. Young boys worked in the breakers, where they pulled pieces of slate from the coal as it went past them on chutes, making such a racket that conversation was impossible and they had to sit there silently all day long. The boys got one to three dollars a week for their work, with few of them having the chance to learn to read or write, and many dying before they had passed from their teens.

The wages of the men and boys, low as they were, were subject to the weather and closing of mines, because of an accident, or a change of ownership. Every now and then, sometimes as a result of reduction of wages, the men went on strike, even though strikes and unions were illegal. "Any agreement, combination, or confederation to increase the price of any vendable commodity, whether labour, merchandizing or anything else," said the court in the Siney-Parks case, "is conspiracy."

Originally, the miners set up the Workingmen's Benevolent Association, but it was destroyed by an unsuccessful strike in 1870 against a thirty per cent wage reduction in the northern fields. This and similar organizations did have one success; they brought about the passage of badly needed inspection laws. Their failures, however, led to the setting up of secret organizations, to protect leaders from being dismissed from their jobs by the operators. The operators, in retaliation, according to Anthony Bimba, an early writer, called the most famous of these organizations the Molly Maguires, charging it with all the riots and murders in the areas. According to Bimba, "After the label itself had been made sufficiently fatal to send a man to the gallows, the mine owners proceeded to fasten this label upon all miners' leaders they wished to get rid of."

Fr D. I. McDermott, of Pottsville, declared in the *Freeman's Journal,* June 30th, 1877, that the Irish miners were mistreated and their resentment led to the disorders. According to Fr McDermott: "The operators and bosses were mostly anti-Catholic and anti-Irish. They were members of secret societies which, if not professedly, at least practically, were opposed to giving the Irish-Catholic any alternative except to leave the region or to become a hewer of wood and a drawer of water for others."

The biggest operator was Franklin B. Gowen, lawyer and former district attorney in Schuylkill County, who became owner of about 125,000 acres of the most valuable coal lands in the country, and president of the Philadelphia and Reading Railroad Company. Gowen told the Pennsylvania legislature that he had tried to treat his workers "fairly and liberally," but all his attempts "to establish friendly relations" had been impossible "on account of the character of the political agitators who appear among them." Gowen said these men make it their business "to destroy confidence . . . to create trouble . . . to sow dissension."

To collect evidence, Gowen called on the Pinkerton Detective Agency, which chose James McParlan, a native of the county of Armagh, in Ulster. He was about twenty-nine when he undertook the mission. He looked Irish, had an unmistakable brogue, and an ability to sing and dance. He took the name of James McKenna, and assumed the identity of a miner from Colorado, looking for work in the East.

McKenna, as instructed, went to Port Clinton, a small town on the line dividing Berks and Schuylkill counties, made friends with the Irish workers, joined the Ancient Order of Hibernians, and got into their inner circles as one of them. Henry J. Browne, in *The Catholic Church and the Knights of Labor,* charges Pinkerton detectives, such as McKenna, with even taking "part in planning the murders, arson and beatings." Bishop James E. Wood of Philadelphia and several other Pennsylvania bishops condemned the A. O. H.

The first trials for assaults and murders resulting from the spying activities began in 1876. Jurors "were picked carefully to exclude the influences of sympathy or fear," reported the Philadelphia *Inquirer*. "Catholics and those residing in isolated places were not used." Since the Civil War stories of draft defiance by Irish miners were still fresh in the minds of the people, the special prosecutor, General Allbright, appeared in full military uniform during the trials, and the charge was made that the Mollies led a fight against the draft in Schuylkill County. The statement was apparently successful, although both the Irish and Germans furnished more troops to the federal armies in proportion to their numbers than did native-born northerners. The picture of draft opposition was provided when poor miners, unable to pay the customary bounty to escape service, were "torn from their homes, wives and children" by the military. At one time, October 16th, 1876, nineteen convicted Molly Maguires were brought into the Pottsville courtroom, chained together, to be sentenced. On June 21st, 1877, nine men were hanged in a single day. With them died the Molly Maguires.

The next secret organization of workingmen to arouse attention was the Knights of Labor, founded by Uriah Smith Stevens and other Philadelphia garment workers. The Knights had a membership of fifty thousand in 1878, when Terrence V. Powderly, a Catholic, became Grand Master. By 1885, after a successful defiance of Jay Gould in the Southwest railroad strike, the membership was some seven hundred thousand. Powderly was born in Carbondale, Pennsylvania, of Irish parents, in 1849, the eleventh of twelve children. His diaries show that he was active as a leader in the Machinists' Union, literary and debating clubs, Scranton parish groups, temperance meetings and other activities. He was a practising Catholic.

The Knights were at first a secret organization "hedged about with the impenetrable veil of ritual, sign, grip, and password, so that no spy of the boss can find his way into the lodge room to betray his fellows". They believed that all workers should band together in one organization, advocated public ownership of railways, waterworks, gas plants, and cooperative institutions for production and distribution. The Pittsburgh convention in 1881 called for laws for incorporation of trade unions, limitation of child labour, uniform apprentice laws, an enforceable eight-hour day, and wages in lawful money. The second convention in Cleveland added free trade.

The secrecy and neo-Masonic rituals of the Knights alarmed Catholic conservatives, and in 1881, Powderly himself persuaded the organization to become public, change its ritual and substitute a word of honour for the secret oath. Criticism did not abate. Allan Pinkerton in 1878 said he was convinced that the Knights are "an amalgamation of the Molly Maguires and the Commune". One industrialist warned a Catholic priest that the growth of the Knights meant that the United States will experience "scenes not less terrible than those committed by the Commune in Paris." In 1875,

Archbishop James Roosevelt Bayley of Baltimore said, "The idea [of labour organizations] is communistic, and no Catholic with any idea of the spirit of his religion will encourage them."

In Canada, conservative Archbishop Tashereau of Quebec appealed in 1883 for a judgement from Rome. A year later, a decree condemning the union in Canada was granted, and Catholic members of the organization were permitted to receive the sacraments only if they promised to avoid violence and injustice, to abstain from any oath of complete obedience to the society, and to withdraw if instructed to do so by the Holy See or their bishop.

Archbishop Gibbons was of the opinion, and so informed the Third Plenary Council of the United States hierarchy at Baltimore (1884), that the Roman decree was of local, Canadian application and not binding on the United States. Gibbons worked hard to prevent a further decree from Rome definitively condemning the Knights of Labor; half a million Catholics were members and the risk of alienating them from the Church was to be avoided at all costs. "Labour has rights as well as capital," he argued.

In Rome, where he had gone to receive the cardinal's hat (1887), with the help of Archbishops Keane and Ireland, and with some assistance from Cardinal Manning, Gibbons busied himself with the Knights' case, pointing out that strictly they were no longer a secret society and insisting on the danger of alienating the workers from the Church.

Although by the time that the decision came from Rome the Knights of Labor were rapidly decreasing in numbers and not long afterwards were swallowed up by the newly formed American Federation of Labor, the issue was of wider importance for it showed that the Church had allied herself with the cause of the workers. This was to be of lasting influence in the U.S.A., and foreshadowed the definite teaching on the rights and obligations of the workers in Leo XIII's great charter *Rerum Novarum*.

America's workers greatly needed the application of the

principles so clearly laid down in the document; it was to be some decades before this benefit was granted to them. Housing conditions remained very bad. In the large cities like Chicago in 1883-4, there were "tenements into which thousands of workingmen are huddled, wholesale violation of all the rules for drainage, plumbing, light, ventilation and safety . . . neglect of all the laws of health, horrible conditions of sewers. . . ." (Citizens Association of Chicago Report).

The yearly unemployment rate ran at a million or more but public assistance was denied to those who would not take the "ironclad oath" that they were not, never had been and never would be members of a union. Trade unions were still unrecognized by law and injunctions were regularly granted by the courts to stop strikes, the workers' only weapon.

Cardinal Gibbons and others spoke out for recognition of the rights of labour to organize, but he did not speak in full agreement with all the Catholic religious and lay leaders. Fr Edward McGlynn, of New York, was outstanding as a Catholic champion of Henry George, the advocate of radical land laws, but he also spoke strongly against those priests and bishops who continued to "tell the hard-working poor to be content with their lot and hope for good times in heaven".

At the same time *Rerum Novarum* (1891) was not being taught in the seminaries and fear of socialism was general on the part of the Catholic clergy. In these final years of the nineteenth century many Catholics advocated compulsory arbitration. Three out of four speakers at the 1893 Catholic Congress in Chicago supported compulsory government arbitration.

At the turn of the century, although it could be said that American Catholic workers, unlike those in France and Italy, had not been lost to the Church, there still remained much to be done: indeed only a beginning had been made.

CHAPTER VIII

THE TWENTIETH CENTURY

ENGLAND

Catholics continue to be a minority in England today, but their proportion is increasing. The main reason is immigration. The Irish arrived at the rate of 40,000 a year after World War II, though improved economic conditions on the isle cut this in half in the 'sixties. Italians, Poles and Spaniards also arrived in their thousands, but of these, only the Poles tended to remain as citizens. It was estimated in 1963 that there were 3,730,000 Catholics in England, compared with an estimated thirty million baptized members of the Church of England.

The descendants of Irish immigrants greatly outnumbered the native Catholics. They crowded the cities, like Liverpool and Manchester, and concentrated in overgrown villages, where they lived, wrote C. F. C. Masterman in 1909, in "mazes of little two-storeyed cottages, the furnaces, the great streets, a few public buildings, all set in a background of greyness, in a devastated landscape, under a grey sky". Their pennies built the churches around which ranked their terraced houses. The third and much smaller group were the professionals, doctors, lawyers, teachers and writers, many of them converts. The last were to form the backbone of the movement by which English Catholics and non-Catholics learned about and acted upon the social teachings of the Church.

Herbert Vaughan, the third archbishop of Westminster, prepared the way for the movement that was to come. So did Cardinal Manning, of course, by virtue of his inspiration and activities. Cardinal Vaughan wandered through the slums of Manchester and was appalled. Before a public meeting in the Salford Town Hall in 1890, he held up a map of the borough. On it, the death rate was shown in dark and shaded areas. The rotten blotches and patches, he said, reminded him of the body of a leper. Improvement of the housing would save thousands of lives a year, he asserted.

The Cardinal called upon employers in 1896 to provide for the old age or sickness of their employees. Dominant selfishness, he said, was the enemy of both capital and labour, and religion alone could curb this selfishness. In 1899 at the annual meeting of the Catholic Truth Society, Cardinal Vaughan declared that millions of people were sheltered far worse than the cattle and horses of many squires. Nearly a million of the London poor should be rehoused. Old age pensions, he declared, should be sufficient to keep recipients in frugal comfort. The injunctions of people like Cardinal Vaughan resulted in little action among the wealthy, according to Leslie A. St L. Toke and Virginia Crawford in 1907. Toke declared that the reason was that these people were "unfamiliar with Catholic social principles as taught by popes and saints and theologians".

Fr Charles Dominic Plater (1875-1921) made "A Plea for Catholic Social Action" in an article signed only by the letter "P" in the February, 1908 issue of the *Month,* the Jesuit review. He deplored the apathy of Catholics and proposed as a remedy that experts be engaged to produce a sound social literature, that these works be discussed in study and workmen's clubs, both of which would aim at producing Catholic labour leaders and speakers. At another time, Plater reminded the clergy and the educated laity that they had been called upon by Leo XIII to "go to the people". The workers are being allured by materialist literature, while Catholics are idle.

One reason that Catholics who could take a lead in social action did not do so, was their fear of socialism. Socialism, to most people in England in those days, meant Marxism, and Leo XIII had condemned it. What was more, Marxian and anti-Christian influences had penetrated the British labour movement.

Against this background, Fr Plater announced the formation "of a Catholic society for social study" at the twenty-fifth annual conference of the Catholic Truth Society in Manchester in 1909. Earlier, at a luncheon presided over by Mgr Henry Parkinson, the Catholic Social Guild had been born. Fr Plater had called upon Parkinson; the former Fabian socialist and Balliol man, Toke; James Britten, a convert, who had founded the Catholic Truth Society in 1884; Virginia Crawford, who had been received into the Church twenty years earlier by Cardinal Manning; Margaret Fletcher, the convert daughter of a vicar; Bertrand Devas, a son of the Catholic economist, Charles Stanton Devas (1848-1906), who, when he died in 1906, was described by the *Economic Journal* as distinguished among writers on political economy in that he had considered the subject from the Catholic point of view.

"Economics must be essentially ethical, the application of the moral law in particular departments of human life," Devas said. Catholic sympathy, he declared, should be with the workers in their efforts to improve their lot. He took the position that farm workers and small businesses were especially entitled to the active concern of Catholics. Devas contributed to clear thinking about socialism. He objected to the opposition to welfare legislation on the ground that it was socialist. This was a way, he said, not of discrediting, but promoting socialism. The workman must not be told only that Leo XIII condemned socialism; he must be informed that the pope condemned the abuses of violence and communism. Devas contended that the socialists, by their efforts to endow the mill hand, farm hand and slum dweller with their own home, to put an end to usury, monopoly, and ruthless business competition, are the true pupils of Leo. In a talk, "Plain Words on Socialism," delivered before the

Catholic Truth Society of Scotland, just a few months before his death, he pointed out that certain forms of municipal socialism, or municipal ownership of utilities, may be justified under certain circumstances.

The first president of the Guild was Mgr Henry Parkinson (1852-1924), rector of Oscott College, on the outskirts of Birmingham. Even before the turn of the century he had given a course of social studies to his seminarians because of what he had seen as a curate in the slums of Birmingham. Others who at that time were showing an active interest in social questions were the Benedictines Abbot Snow, Bishop Hedley and Dom J. B. McLaughlin of Dowlais; among the Jesuits, besides those already mentioned, were Frs Joseph Rickaby and Joseph Keating. Fr Cuthbert, the Capuchin, had published a book on *Catholic Ideals in Social Life* in 1904. The great Dominican, Fr Vincent McNabb, was heard in May, 1907, preaching a course of social sermons in Westminster Cathedral. In 1908, he began at Leicester the career of social and civic work and contact with Protestants in social matters that was only interrupted by World War I.

Mgr Parkinson edited and prefaced a volume of articles on social subjects for the Catholic Truth Society before he became president of the Guild, but in urging Catholics to take part in social work, he admitted that a library of social manuals had yet to be written.

The Catholic Truth Society, which had already done important work in this field, published the new series for the Guild. It included copies of the papal social encyclicals and discussions of *Catholic Principles of Social Reform, English Economics and Catholic Ethics, Practical Social Reform, The Living Wage, Trade Unionism* and other subjects. In addition, the Guild put out a series of leaflets on similar subjects; yearbooks, which sold for sixpence and were no bigger than the popular paperbacks; a series of *Catholic Studies in Social Reform,* treating subjects like poverty, sweatshop labour, housing and social service; a quarterly bulletin, which provided information on Catholic social progress in England and elsewhere, and, its successor in 1921, the *Christian Democrat,* a monthly magazine.

Catholic Book Notes, a publication of the Catholic Truth Society, in its issue of January 10th, 1910, set forth the objective of the Guild in these words: "If the great social changes, which are coming in this country, are to be made in harmony with Catholic principles, Catholics must make these principles known. The object of the Guild is to stimulate in Catholics a greater sense of the urgency of the situation, to induce them to learn the Catholic standpoint in these matters, and to impart their knowledge to others."

By means of study clubs, correspondence courses and a school examination board, together with the publication of further manuals and pamphlets, the Catholic Social Guild contrived to spread its influence far and wide in the country, reaching convent schools, seminaries, and many of the Catholic workers in the industrial North especially. But the effect of all this action, widespread though it was, must not be exaggerated. In 1928, Fr Leo O'Hea, S.J., noted that except for the seminaries and the girls in convent schools, the Catholic middle class in general was not informed about the Church's social teaching.

In 1920, the Guild held its first summer school at Oxford. This was so successful that the school became an annual affair. In 1921 Fr Plater's hope of a Catholic Workers' College at Oxford was realized. "It is not enough," he had written in 1909, "for Catholic workers to listen . . . to other people's lectures. They must train themselves to lecture. Otherwise, how can we possibly expect them to be alert in the defence of Catholic principles? How can we expect them to be even moderately interested in the Catholic position?"

Fr Plater himself was not to see the college come into being, for he died early in 1921. The college opened in October 1921 as a living memorial to Fr Plater. Fr Leo O'Hea, S.J., who was first in charge of it, was the dominating figure not only there but over the whole Guild for the next thirty years. The first three students were all workers: a textile operator and treasurer of the Preston Trades Council, a sheet-metal worker from Preston and an engine driver of the Great Western Railway from South Wales.

In the years that followed, the College and Guild grew, attracting persons like Alice Meynell, the poet, in the early years, G. K. Chesterton in 1924 and later, as a really hard worker, Barbara Ward. Workers were joining the British Trade Union Congress. "Just as there is no reason why a Catholic should be found in the Communist Party, there is no reason why he should not be a member of an English trade union," said the Guild's historian, Georgiana Putnam McEntee. George Woodcock, general secretary of the TUC since 1960, pointed out that four members of the Congress' general council are Catholics: Sir William Carron, of the Amalgamated Engineers, Britain's second largest union; Sir Tom O'Brien, of the Theatrical and Cinema Workers; Joe O'Hagan, of the Blast Furnace Workers, and himself.

Britain has no Catholic trade unions. It had an organization called the National Conference of Catholic Trade Unions, but that was not a union, merely an association of Catholics who were members of trade unions. The first meeting of the C.T.U. was held at Manchester in 1908. It opposed the annual resolution in favour of secular education at the TUC annual meeting, but never successfully. When the Labour Party was formed, the C.T.U. took the position that no Catholic should be a member, but when Archbishop Keating of Liverpool, and other members of the hierarchy, said that it was the duty of Catholics not to leave the party, but purge it, the C.T.U. in the early 'twenties ceased to exist.

Ramsay MacDonald, leader of the Labour Party, said in the early years of the party:

> The Labour Party is not socialist. It is a union of socialist and trade union bodies for immediate political work—the Social Democratic Party having joined it first, but after a year's cooperation having returned to its isolation in 1901. But it is the only political form which evolutionary socialism can take in a country with the political traditions and methods

of Great Britain. Under British conditions, a Socialist Party is the last, not the first form of the socialist movement in politics.

Fr Vincent McNabb wrote in high praise of both Mac-Donald and the "new socialism." He asserted that there were many forms of resemblance between Leo XIII's ideas and many of those of the Labour Party. He urged Catholics to disregard labels. Fr Cuthbert, O.F.M.Cap., in a pamphlet issued by the Catholic Social Guild, examined the basic principles of the Labour Party and found them in accordance with Catholic doctrine.

Difficulties arose within the Guild when the Labour Party adopted a new constitution calling for common ownership of the means of production. The *Christian Democrat,* under the editorship of Fr Paul Crane, S.J., was suspicious of nationalization, and maintained it was not necessary for full employment. Fr Crane saw the Welfare State as violative of subsidiarity. As Fr William F. Ryan, S.J., in *Social Order* for June, 1955, interpreted Fr Crane's thinking: "Not only does State welfare threaten to dehumanize the citizen, but it has a particular bias against the family. It not merely dulls a father's initiative by excessive taxation; it renders his efforts to support his family less worthwhile by distributing benefits to individual family members on an impersonal basis."

During the period after World War II, Guild membership began a slow decline. Many members of the Guild did not agree with Fr Crane, and Guild publications on each side of the argument marked "This is written to promote discussion. The Guild is not committed to any views here expressed" did not temper their attitude. The fact was that many British Catholics supported the Labour Party. At the same time, J. M. Cleary argued in his history of the Catholic Social Guild, "the Guild was the most suitable Catholic body to provide constructive criticism of the greatest social experiment Britain has ever undertaken. The Guild did not seize the opportunity sufficiently, and in the distraction of the Welfare State controversy, what little practical work was published . . . was overlooked, and continues to be forgotten."

In any case, although the Catholics in Britain remain a minority, they have become an informed, respected and influential body, and most of the credit goes to those zealous and persevering members of the Catholic Social Guild. They have been valiant in the implementation of their belief that God's will must be done on earth.

FRANCE

The twentieth century in France witnessed Communist domination of the nation's largest trade union federation and the continued valiant efforts of French Catholics to win back the workers, through Catholic trade unions, priest-workers and Catholic social education and action.

In 1884, urged by Catholic leaders and others, the French Republic voted the right of freedom of association, which recognized the fact that unions existed. French employers, however, refused to accept the law, and for two generations they dismissed and blacklisted trade unionists, used spies and *agents provocateurs,* and set up company unions. During this time, France had a National Federation of Trade Unions, and the Federation of the Bourses, but both gave way to the General Federation of Labour, *Conféderation Générale du Travail,* the CGT, which was founded in 1895. The CGT, about the time of World War I, had a left-wing minority, with its strongest base among the Paris metal workers. After the war, the CGT endorsed U.S. President Wilson's Fourteen Points, and later supported the League of Nations and the International Labour Organization. The federation leader, Léon Jouhaux, was appointed to the Peace Conference delegation.

Before *Rerum Novarum,* in 1887 a Brother of the Christian Schools united the Catholic white-collar workers of Paris in the *Syndicat des Employés du Commerce et de l'Industrie.* In 1891, the first textile workers' union was formed by Catholics in the North. In 1919 came the French federation of Catholic workers, *Conféderation Française des Travailleurs Chrétiens,* the CFTC. It was not at first in a strong position; in 1920, of its 140,000 claimed members only 65,000 paid dues, even though these dues were minimal.

The CFTC differed from the CGT in that it did not emphasize the class struggle, but sought social justice and economic democracy through cooperation with employers and the State. The CFTC did not, however, abandon the right to strike. It was active with the CGT in the post-World War I strikes in clothing, banking, and in some textile and metallurgical centres, but it opposed general strikes, such as that in 1920, as political. In 1927, the Young Catholic Workers, *Jeunesse Ouvriére Chrétienne,* the JOC, was formed as a link between Catholics and workers, and also as a training ground for CFTC leadership.

Earlier, in 1904, the *Semaine sociale* was organized in France as a means of enabling leading Catholic experts on social and economic problems to instruct students and others in Catholic social principles. These annual "weeks" have been held with increasing success since their first organization.

The *Association catholique,* which began publication in 1895, urged protection of women and children in factories, limitation of the work week, wages "sufficient for the support of an average family and for the maintenance of benefit funds to provide for expenses resulting from accidents, sickness, old age, etc." *Association catholique* was the precursor of *Action Populaire,* which published a series of cheap pamphlets, three a month, each about thirty pages long, on Catholic social teaching.

In 1920, following the end of World War I, the CGT, involved in the Communist war against trade unionists and socialists who did not follow Moscow direction, called a general strike. The strike cost the CGT considerable membership; its two million at the beginning of the year had shrunk to 600,000 at the end. The fight between the left and right in the federation resulted from formation of the Red International of Labour Unions, which opposed the moderate, socialist national trade union centre, and the International Federation of Trade Unions, of which Jouhaux was a founder and vice-president. Communist domination of the CGT did not come about, however, until after World War II.

During World War II, the Vichy government dissolved the CGT, the CFTC, and the national steel and coal trade associations. The leaders of the trade union movements joined General Charles de Gaulle's Free French, sent delegates to London and to Algiers. Workers were active in the resistance, in the fight against forced labour under the Nazis, in propaganda, the intelligence network, sabotage, and in the Maquis. The number of forced labourers sent to Germany was estimated at 600,000, with French priests like the Jesuit Fr Henri Perrin going too, concealing their priesthood, anxious to minister to their fellow prisoners.

When liberation came, both trade unionists and Catholic priests had won new prestige. By September, 1945, the CGT claimed 5,454,000 members, and the CFTC three quarters of a million. Just before liberation and immediately afterwards, the CGT called upon the CFTC to merge, offering them proportional representation in the leadership. The CFTC executive board refused, citing disagreements on political action, women's work, and the parochial schools. The CFTC did cooperate with the CGT in seeking and gaining nationalization of coal mines, gas and electricity production and distribution, the Bank of France, the four largest deposit banks, the thirty-four largest insurance companies, and the large Renault automobile company, whose head, Louis Renault, had been accused of collaboration. Boards of directors represented a majority of the CGT, a minority of the CFTC, consumers, and the government.

Both federations also worked together in increasing family allowances, health, maternity, sickness, and old-age insurance benefits. Workmen's compensation was made part of the public system. Workers' representatives were given a preponderant place on the social security administrative board, on the theory that control should be in the hands of the insured. Labour-management plant committees were established by law, with the committees given control of plant social welfare work and consultative powers in production and economic decisions. The shop steward system was restored, with elections required in all plants with more than ten workers. Jouhaux, who had long advocated a National Economic Council, was elected its president when it was set up, with other CGT and CFTC union heads as members. Representatives of both federations were also on the Council of the Monnet Planning Commission for the nation's economic modernization and re-equipment. With the Communists cooperating in reconstruction De Gaulle, in late 1944, permitted the party head, Maurice Thorez, to return from Moscow. He had been condemned as an army deserter in 1939, and fled the country.

After Thorez' return, the Communists began to take over the CGT as their main base of power. By April, 1946, they were able to vote a four-to-one majority in convention. In the confused and critical months of 1944-45, reports Val Lorwin, "Alone of the resistance bodies, political parties, and union groups, the Communists knew what they wanted and moved firmly to get it".

The principal opposition to the Communists within the CGT came from a group known as *Force Ouvrière* (FO), led by Jouhaux who had been the undisputed general secretary until the Communists elected Benoît Frachon as co-general secretary. Not all, or even perhaps most, of the members of the CGT are Communists. Some workers joined the CGT because of personal attachment to local leaders, sentimental attachment to "the old CGT", or because the CGT already represented their fellow workers. The CGT has made the claim, with some justification, that it includes more Catholics than the CFTU and more Socialists than the FO. The French hierarchy recognized the practical difficulty facing some workers, since the CGT is everywhere and that is not true of the CFTU and the FO. They preferred that workers should belong to the Catholic unions but realized that circumstances sometimes require otherwise.

The CGT is strongest, as is the Communist party, in the working-class districts, the "red belt" around Paris. Another area of strength is the coal, metallurgical and textile region of the north. A third is along the eastern Mediterranean coast, the ports of Marseilles and Toulon, shipbuilding and navy yards and the tourist region of the Riviera.

Principal strongholds of the CFTU are to be found among the traditionally Catholic people of Alsace, in the north (cotton and wool textiles), parts of Brittany and Savoy and the industrial concentrations of the south-east (Lyons, Grenoble, Saint-Étienne). In Paris and other cities its members are white-collar workers employed in commerce and industry.

Because in recent years many non-Catholics, including Moslems, have joined CFTC unions, in 1947 the opening of its declaration of principles was changed from "the social doctrine defined in the encyclical *Rerum Novarum*" to the broader context of the "principles of Christian morality". It also asserted its independence of "all outside groups, political or religious". As a result the designation Catholic was dropped from the name of the federation so that it is now the *Conféderation Française Démocratique du Travail* (French Democratic Confederation of Workers). A group of younger members of the CFTC have been leading the movement against the confessional character of the federation, and in favour of industrial unionism, political neutrality and union with the FO. Developments of this kind would also probably make the French non-Communist force a realistic challenge to the CGT.

Meanwhile, the comparative strength of the Communist and non-Communist trade union forces in France is changing drastically. In 1945, the CGT claimed almost six million members; today, according to social security elections, the CGT has only 3,500,000. In 1945, the CFTC and FO each claimed a million members. Today, also according to the social security elections, the CFDT (former CFTC) has 1,600,-000 and FO 1,200,000. CGT is still dominant, but the former six million to two million has been changed to 3,500,000 to 2,800,000. The next few years may well be historic and important not only to France, but to the world.

Among French efforts to bring the worker back into the Church, none has been more dramatic and, for a time, more hopeful than the priest-worker movement. During both World Wars, the French clergy served as stretcher bearers and attendants of the sick and wounded at the front, as chaplains and simple soldiers; in World War II they got themselves into the forced labour camps in Germany. They lived, worked and suffered with their fellow men, had the same needs and anxieties, learned what brings men together, rather than what divides them.

With few practising Catholics among the workers of the crowded industrial areas around Paris and elsewhere—one report showed only four Catholics among 19,000 workers in one industrial complex—two Jocist chaplains of Paris, Abbés Henri Godin and Yvan Daniel submitted a memorandum to Cardinal Suhard, archbishop of Paris, on the almost complete dechristianization of the working masses, and the need, as they saw it, of making such parts of France "mission country". This was on March 5th, 1943.

As chaplain of the Young Christian Workers, Abbé Godin realized that he was not reaching the vast pagan world surrounding the tiny islands of Catholics. Godin was born on April 13th, 1906, in a small French village, and entered the seminary as early as he could. After he had returned home for the holidays after his first months at the seminary, an old friend told him, "You've changed, Henri. You don't belong to us any more".

Godin was shocked. He realized he had begun to think of his former companions, not as "us", but "they". He prayed for "them", instead of saying, "Lord Jesus, workmen like us". He asked another former companion about himself and others who went to the seminary. "They're bourgeois now. They don't care about the working classes," he was informed. "There ought to be a seminary for workmen where they'd stay workmen when they become priests. All priests are bourgeois."

Godin pointed out that he had to obtain an education, as must all priests. He argued that this did not make him bourgeois, but nevertheless, from that moment on, he was concerned. That was why he interested himself in the Jocists.

One of the Jocist workers wrote: "He was not a priest friendly to the people; he was simply one of the people. We felt him so close to us in the whole of his life." Cardinal Suhard, like Abbé Godin, was well aware of the spiritual needs of French workers. In 1942, before he called upon Godin and Daniel to write the report, the cardinal had started the *Mission de France* at Lisieux. There he had already begun training missionaries for bishops who wanted them. Their training at the seminary included six months' work in a factory or on a farm, so that before ordination the young priests would learn something of the world they were to evangelize.

In September, 1943, Cardinal Suhard ordered the publication of 100,000 copies of the Godin-Daniel memorandum, under the title *France Pagan?* On January 13th, 1944, the Cardinal formally launched the Mission with these words: "The primary object of the Mission to Paris is to convert the heathen. Its secondary object is to demonstrate to the Christian community that it needs to adopt a new attitude."

A few days later, on January 17th, Abbé Godin, just 37, was accidentally asphyxiated in his little flat, three floors up, in the Rue Ganneron. He had been complaining of headaches for months; no one realized until too late that there was a leak in the little gas heater that stood in the bedroom that also served as study and reception room.

Meanwhile, one priest asked for permission to go to work. Permission was granted for one month, then for a second. Others followed his example. The move was underway for priests to be "a worker among workers, as Christ was a man among men, of linking one's destiny to their destiny, one's life to their life, of being the one among them whose hopes go farther than their hopes." In the provinces, procedures were different. At Marseilles in October, 1945, secular and regular priests set up a "missionary parish." One of this group, Fr Jacques Loew, O.P., had been stevedoring on the docks since 1942, to carry out an economic and sociological study. A similar parish was established at Givors (Rhône) in September, 1946. At Lyons, several priests took jobs at the same time. A team at Limoges was formed in September, 1947, at the request of the local clergy, to take on a task separate from that of the parish. Other teams were formed at Bordeaux, Toulouse, Saint-Étienne and in the north of France; in the Lorraine basin, at Le Havre, and near Nice. Some priests went into mines, some took to the sea, others helped build dams, as well as going into factories.

The priests were to be carefully selected. The greatest care was ordered to be taken to choose priests "who are well balanced physically, intellectually and morally; who possess a sound culture in philosophy and theology and, lastly, who have a fair experience of pastoral work." Some of those selected had been in parishes for five, eight or even eighteen years. Their ages ranged from twenty-eight to fifty-eight, with the average about thirty-five. The archbishop examined some candidates personally.

Priests entered wholly into the lives of the workers. On February 4th, 1951, a priest-worker and former prisoner of war was elected full-time secretary of the metal workers of Paris. Some priest-workers were discharged by employers, who said they wanted no priests in their establishments. In November and December, 1947, priest-workers, most of whom had joined the CGT, because that was where they were needed, took part in the general strikes.

On May 28th, 1952, a Communist organization, the Movement for Peace, called for a popular demonstration against the appointment of U.S. General Ridgway as commander of the North Atlantic Treaty Organization. The CGT entered into the demonstrations, calling upon their members to take part. Tens of thousands of people moved along the main highways leading to Paris and through the city and clashed with the police. At one point, the police opened fire. One person was killed and several wounded. Hundreds were arrested, among them two priest-workers. That evening the French Foreign Office called the office of the Nuncio, who in turn called Rome. That same year, Fr Michael Favreau, dock worker in the port of Bordeaux, took the place of a fellow worker who was ill. It was Fr Favreau's day off. A crane landed on him, crushed his chest, and he died. Three thousand dockers and port workers were at his funeral. In Sagny, a Paris slum district, the destitute were coming daily to the house of Fr Pierre, with their housing problems, complaints about wages, their personal anguish. Some of the workers were getting as little as forty dollars a month, and were exploited by their employers and landlords.

The French experience with priest-workers was mixed. Maisie Ward in *Unfinished Business* tells of First Communion Sunday at St Trophime, the Marseilles suburb rejuvenated church. The Sunday was impressive. On one occasion, there were so many children that two Sundays had to be set aside, but, she added, "This would be the last time the bigger boys would come to church, except for their own marriage perhaps, or their own children's First Communion." Many priests were unable to meet the arguments of the Communists. One priest left the Church, married and became the secretary to the local Communist party. Others who were not won over to the Communist line, did become more worker than priest. Even the famous Fr Perrin mouthed the party line, "flowing mechanically, if not hypnotically, from his lips".

In September, 1953, the Apostolic Nuncio called a meeting of bishops and superiors. "Work is not the danger," he said, "but this collaboration with the Communists." On November 15th, 1953, the decision from Rome was made public. "After ten years of existence, the priest-worker experience as it has developed up to now cannot continue. The Church therefore demands:

"Priest-workers should be especially chosen by their bishops.
"They should devote only a limited time to work.
"They should leave temporal responsibilities to laymen.
"They should play their part in the life of the parish."

Seventy-three priests, among them Fr Perrin, refused to obey. They asserted: "We do not think that our life as workers has ever prevented us from continuing loyal to our faith and our priesthood. We cannot see how priests can be forbidden, in the name of the Gospel, to share the condition of millions of oppressed humanity or to be on their side in their struggles."

On January 19th, 1954, the orders were more specific: "Priest-workers are forbidden to work more than three hours a day. They are forbidden to belong to any organization whatsoever, or to accept responsible office therein. They must be attached to a community of priests. They are forbidden to set up a team on the national level."

Priest-workers continue in France according to the new rules. The seminary, which was closed by the 1954 decision, was reopened at Pontigny, and there are now some 400 *Mission de France* priests, of whom 350 have been trained at the seminary. They work in little groups of from three to eight men.

France, once considered a Catholic country, is today estimated to be twenty-five per cent Catholic, based on attendance at Mass and the sacraments. Paris is about fifteen per cent Catholic, the industrial areas around the city about five per cent. The Church has won over many of the nation's intellectuals, and has most active liberal Catholic Action groups, but the workers are still to be won back to the Church.

THE UNITED STATES

John Ryan, one of eleven children born to Irish immigrants, on rich farm land west of Minneapolis, May 25th, 1869, and Peter Ernest Dietz, born of Bavarian immigrant parents, on New York's East Side, July 10th, 1878, were the outstanding priestly champions of the worker in the United States in the first part of the twentieth century. Each made his different contribution. Father Ryan urged industrial democracy; Father Dietz was a fighter for trade unionism. Ryan enunciated the principles of social justice; Dietz battled in the arena. As Aaron I. Abell says in *American Catholicism and Social Action*, Ryan was the academician and Peter Dietz the organizer of the American Catholic social movement.

Both men sought to rouse others into affirmative action. At St Paul's Seminary, Fr Ryan devoted a fourth of his two-year course in junior moral theology to economic history and political economy. Catholics, Ryan said, were "so preoccupied refuting Socialism and defending the present order, that they go to the opposite extreme, understating the amount of truth in the claims of the Socialists and overstating the rights of property and the advantages of the present system". Ryan pointed out that his own brethren in the seminary got their ideas of social problems mostly from conservative journals hostile to reform. The result: "The bishops who have made any pronouncement in the matter (of the social teaching of the Church) could probably be counted on the fingers of one hand, while the priests who have done so are not more numerous proportionately." Ryan was as critical of the laymen. He spent the rest of his life in training and inspiring clerical and lay leaders.

Dietz was ordained in 1904. As his first assignment, he was placed in charge of Sacred Heart Chapel at Oberlin College. In April, 1906, Fr Dietz challenged the priests of Lorain County, Ohio, to take up their rôles in modern society. The way to defeat Socialism, "which as a protest against existing conditions is justified indeed," Dietz argued, is to better the lot of the worker. He recommended Catholic loan associations, building associations, Catholic influence upon trades councils, more literature and lecture courses for the enlightenment of the workers, not only on industrial, but also on political problems. Before adjourning, the priests agreed to assist the laymen of the county in forming a federation which would affiliate with the American Federation of Catholic Societies, formed in Cincinnati in 1901. Fr Dietz worked out a plan for the study of labour, socialism and other current subjects.

On Labour Day, 1906, in Elyria, Ohio, Fr Dietz called on workers to form unions. However, he added, speaking of Socialism, "beware of agitators and idle theorists who continually appeal to the future because they have no share in the present."

The Socialist factions in the United States had joined in 1901 into the Socialist party of America, stating as their aim the establishment of a cooperative commonwealth, to be attained by peaceful political and parliamentary action. Although Eugene V. Debs obtained nearly nine hundred thousand votes in 1912, the party won its successes in electing a congressman, mayors in several important cities and many local officials; and, Norman Thomas was to say later, in educating the American people to needed social reforms.

The Socialist's paper, *The Appeal to Reason,* was furnished free to members of some unions. Socialist Sunday schools were set up in almost every important city to teach the child to "realize the class struggle and his own part in it." Catechisms and a magazine, *The Little Socialist,* served as textbooks. Catholic priests like Fr Thomas McGrady of Kentucky and Fr Thomas J. Hagerty of Chicago supported the Socialist cause. Such Catholics were embarrassed when J. A. Wayland began to denounce Catholicism in *The Appeal to Reason,* despite the protests of religiously tolerant Socialists.

Wayland launched the violently anti-Catholic paper, *The Menace*, in 1912.

The National Association of Manufacturers, formed in 1895 to promote foreign trade and high tariffs, proposed a simple answer—the end of trade unions. In 1903, David M. Parry, NAM President, informed the New Orleans convention that "the principles and demands of organized labour are absolutely untenable to those believing in the individualistic social order. . . . The greatest danger lies in the recognition of the union."

Some members of unions were Socialist. In 1909, Fr Dietz estimated that ten per cent of the members of American Federation of Labor unions were Socialist. In 1912, the Socialist candidate, Max Hayes, who opposed Samuel Gompers as president, won support from one third of the convention delegates. But Gompers himself and practically all of the other AFL leaders were violently anti-Socialist. They had seen what happened in Europe and they wanted none of it.

Fr Ryan's first important book, *A Living Wage: Its Ethical and Economic Aspects* (1906), did not deal with Socialism, referring to it only in a footnote. Every man, Ryan argued, because he is "endowed by nature, or rather, by God, with the rights that are requisite to a reasonable development of his personality," has a natural right to share in the earth's products. In an industrial society, this right takes the form of a living wage, "a decent livelihood." The employer has the obligation to pay a living wage, Ryan said, and he is released from this obligation only if he is unable to do so. He cannot, however, put his right to a profit or an investor's right to his interest, ahead of the rights of the worker. Ryan asserted that the State has the obligation to see that all employers pay a living wage. In the meantime, minimum wages should be paid for public services and on work done by contract for the government, by all "industries of a monopolistic character" such as railroads, telephone and express companies. He recommended indirect methods such as an

eight-hour day, public housing, and old-age pensions, with
the costs to be paid out of increased inheritance taxes and a
graduated income tax. Ryan analyzed current costs of living
for an average family, suggested $600 as the minimum for
decent living in any American city, and pointed out that
about sixty per cent of America's industrial force fell below
that level in 1906.

In his book, Ryan also called for laws to restrict the labour
of women and children, legalization of picketing, and boy-
cotts; conciliation and arbitration of labour-management disputes by state and national boards with conciliatory powers,
relief of unemployment by State employment bureaus, and
social insurance. Provision should also be made against sickness and accident. The State should protect the consumer
against extortionate prices, and to this end, there should be
public ownership of natural monopolies, including mines
and forests; rigid control of monopolies not based on natural
advantage; taxation of future increases in land values; and
prohibition of speculation on the exchanges.

Meanwhile, Fr Dietz, after having shown himself to be an
unusually enthusiastic defender of social justice at the convention of the German Catholic Central Verein in Cleveland,
in 1908, was made editor of the English edition of the organization's paper. The Verein agreed with Dietz on the importance of labour in any social reform programme. He had
declared:

> If Socialism succeeds in America, it will be because labour-
> unionism has failed. . . . Therefore, the Catholic has a most
> important and responsible share in the industrial readjust-
> ment of society. By his intelligent, Christian membership he
> will be the only solid guarantee that the labour union will
> not become socialistic, but the keystone of a social reform
> that will remove the most distressing features of the social
> problem as they confront us today.

In 1909, at Oberlin, Dietz established his first labour
school, a social institute that offered a series of lectures on
the trade union movement and its special significance for

Catholic workers. In September of that year, students came from as far as Philadelphia, New York, Brooklyn, Buffalo, Cleveland, Columbus, Cincinnati, Chicago, Dubuque and St Paul. They were clergymen, editors, trade unionists and social workers.

In 1909, while attending the Toronto convention of the American Federation of Labor, Dietz heard the Rev Charles Stelzle address the delegates. Stelzle, as the fraternal delegate of the Federal Council of Churches in America, had the privilege of a seat in the convention, and spoke in the name of a large number of U.S. Protestants. Dietz resolved that a Catholic fraternal delegate must somehow attend the next AFL convention. Meanwhile, he organized Catholics at the convention for Sunday Mass in St Michael's in Toronto, and set up an organization of Catholic trade unionists, the Militia of Christ for Social Service.

The American Federation of Catholic Societies named Fr Dietz a delegate to that convention. He agreed with Cardinal Gibbons and others that Catholic trade unions should not be set up in the United States, but the Militia of Christ for Social Service was different; it operated within the established labour movement. Samuel Gompers introduced Fr Dietz at the St Louis convention as the fraternal delegate of the AFCS. Dietz told the convention that the AFCS, representing over three million men of all nationalities, "holds out to the trade union movement the hand of fellowship and support", believing that the AFL "offers a safe, real, constructive, sane and Christian solution to many of our social problems." The Militia was set up as a permanent organization at the conclusion of the convention.

Fr Dietz continually urged the necessity of Catholic workers' knowing the social principles of the Church and the means to put them into practice. He said: "Every Catholic trade unionist must regard it as his sacred duty to be present at the meetings of his trade union and to represent with manly ability the Christian point of view." But Fr Dietz was not without his troubles. One of his most frequent concerns was the fairly common habit of building Catholic churches, schools and other buildings with non-union labour. As the result of a Knights of Columbus clubhouse put up in Milwaukee with non-union labour, the Milwaukee Building Trades Council passed a resolution barring from AFL conventions fraternal delegates representing religious societies, since they were unwilling to "assist and cooperate in the establishment of trade union conditions, for the workers in the various industries, and especially in those over which they had full power to act". Peter Dietz was obliged to give up his work. Various attempts were made to find him a post, but without success, and he ended his days as pastor of a small parish on the outskirts of Milwaukee.

Philip Murray, later president of the CIO, said of Dietz: "He strongly voiced the rights of labour to organize and bargain collectively. This he did at a time when few public figures were willing to do so." Matthew Woll, Dan Tobin, John P. Frey and others said he had a greater influence on the labour movement than any other priest before or since.

During 1912 and 1913, Fr Ryan was engaged in a notable debate on Socialism with Morris Hillquit, in *Everybody's Magazine*. Both agreed on the evils of capitalistic society, and both agreed on the need of intervention by the State, but Hillquit took the materialistic approach and ended with the abolition of private ownership. Ryan repeated the substance of the "Programme of Social Reform by Legislation" that he had first written for the *Catholic World* in 1909, and added the idea that workers share in the ownership of industry. Hillquit called Ryan "probably the most formidable and at the same time the most gratifying opponent it was ever my good fortune to meet in public debate, well informed, painstaking, broadminded, and scrupulously fair."

Ryan's second important book, *Distributive Justice: the Right and Wrong of Our Present Distribution of Wealth*, was published in 1916. It set forth the principles that should govern the proper "distribution of the products of industry among the classes that have taken part in the making of these products"—the landowner, capitalist, entrepreneur, worker. Ryan repeated his living wage theory, adding that the worker is also entitled "to as much more as he can get by competition with the other agents of production and his fellow labourers".

In 1917, with World War I in progress, the bishops of the United States formed the National Catholic War Council, headed by Bishop Muldoon, to coordinate the activities of the Knights of Columbus and other Catholic organizations overseas and at home for the war effort. When the war was over, and other American religious groups made statements, the Administrative Committee of the council felt the need of some kind of Catholic pronouncement. The assignment was given to Fr John F. O'Grady, secretary of the Committee on Reconstruction. O'Grady asked Ryan to prepare the document. Ryan refused at first, but was finally induced to rewrite a few notes he had written on postwar reconstruction for a speech in Louisville. O'Grady was in such a hurry that Ryan put in an immediate five hours on the typewriter.

This was the famous 1919 Bishops' Program for Social Reconstruction, called by Francis L. Broderick, "perhaps the most forward-looking social document ever to come from an official Catholic agency in the United States". The programme called for minimum wage legislation, insurance against unemployment, sickness, disability, and old age; a sixteen-year minimum age limit for working children; legal enforcement of the right of labour to organize; a national employment service; public housing; no general reduction in war-time wages, but a long-term programme of increasing them, not only for the good of the workers, but also to bring about a wider distribution of purchasing power, as the means to prosperity; prevention of excessive profits and income through a regulation of rates which allow the owners of public utilities only a fair return on their actual investment, and through progressive income taxes on inheritance, income, and excess profits; participation of labour in management and a wider distribution of ownership through cooperative enterprises and worker ownership in the stock of corporations; effective control of monopolies, even by the method of government competition if necessary. (All but the proposal of labour participation in management subsequently became fact, and this has not occurred because U.S. labour opposed it.)

The National Catholic Welfare Council, formed late in 1919, took the place of the War Council. It worked through five bureaus, including the Department of Social Action, headed by Ryan. Fr John J. Burke, C.S.P., who had been an active member of the War Council, became general secretary, and Bishop Muldoon chaired the Social Action Department. The NCWC name was changed to National Catholic Welfare Conference in 1923. In the 'twenties, the National Association of Manufacturers opened another attack against organized labour, claiming in a letter "To the Catholic Clergy" that Leo XIII had condemned the closed shop as incompatible with Christianity. Fr Ryan's able and modest assistant, Fr Raymond A. McGowan attacked the N.A.M.'s "American Plan" open-shop campaign, and Ryan called the movement "a hypocritical attempt to cripple the unions under the guise of promoting freedom of contract in industrial relations".

When the Supreme Court declared the child-labour and minimum wage laws unconstitutional, Ryan exploded. He joined a group working on a constitutional amendment, but the fight was hopeless at the time. Ryan also was critical of the AFL, then headed by a man who did not compare with Gompers, William Green. Ryan wanted more militancy, especially in organizing on an industrial basis. Ryan was critical of the Esch-Cummins Act of 1920 because it guaranteed capital a return of five and a half per cent, but did not guarantee workers a living wage. He branded this "immoral discrimination."

When the depression began, Ryan spoke out constantly, largely in *Commonweal*. He said that the depression was President Hoover's bad luck, not his fault, but his failure to act since November, 1929, had destroyed his reputation as a great economist and an effective and courageous leader. Ryan "traced unemployment to the gap between output and buying power" and "advocated higher wages and shorter hours" along with a five-billion dollar federal works programme, while Hoover talked of more credit to business. In the fall of 1930, the Social Action Department released its study of unemployment, which called for higher wages, on the basis of living needs and productivity, shorter hours, collective bargaining, and unemployment insurance.

Dorothy Day, social worker recently converted from Communism, and Peter Maurin, French-born itinerant social philosopher, formed the Catholic Worker movement in 1933. Miss Day and her followers lived among the unemployed poor in the industrial sections of New York and elsewhere. They welcomed the poor into their Houses of Hospitality, combinations of soup kitchens, discussion clubs, and reform centres, and fought their cause in their newspaper, *The Catholic Worker*. They told of the sufferings and exploitation of the unemployed, the homeless and the migrant workers. The Catholic Worker movement is agrarian, pacificist, and anti-industrialist. Some thirty-three Houses of Hospitality were open across the country at one time. Daniel Callahan thinks "the most important result of the Catholic Worker and its allied houses of hospitality was the great number of Catholics who came under its spell and then went on to form new organizations, or to introduce a heightened sense of zeal in older ones".

Members of the Catholic Worker movement walked picket lines, joined and helped organized unions, and otherwise tried to help the trade unions. To systematize these particular activities, Catholic workers in New York, led by John C. Cort, formed the Association of Catholic Trade Unionists in 1937. They took their cue from *Quadragesimo Anno*: "Side by side with . . . trade unions there must always be associations which aim at giving their members a thorough religious and moral training, that these in turn may impart to the labour unions to which they belong the upright spirit

which should direct their entire conduct." ACTU was successful in fighting Communism in unions in New York and
elsewhere, and in eliminating racketeering, such as practised by "paper locals" in New York City, which exploited
the Puerto Ricans.

Young, zealous Catholic boys and girls formed an American branch of the *Jocists,* the Young Christian Workers. In
Chicago, ACTU took a different form, the Catholic Labor
Alliance, which opened its membership to non-unionists
and persons of all faiths who were interested in the furtherance of the principlees of the papal social encyclicals.

The encyclical teachings were also given wide circulation
by the "radio priest," Charles E. Coughlin, of Royal Oaks,
Michigan. Most of the nation listened to him during the
early part of the 'thirties. He was a great Irish orator, and
helped Franklin D. Roosevelt when he was preaching
"Roosevelt or Ruin," but Coughlin was more interested in
monetary inflation and banking control than the New Deal
President, and when his injunctions on these issues were not
heeded, he posed as the martyr of a misunderstood cause.
In 1936, Coughlin formed his own party, with North Dakota
Congressman William Lemke as candidate for President. I in-
terviewed him at this time, finding that he mouthed quotations from his radio speeches as answers to questions. Ryan
meanwhile had been associated with the New Deal. General
Hugh S. Johnson, the administrator of the National Recovery
Administration, named the priest-professor to a three-man
Industrial Appeals Board to hear the complaints of small
manufacturers who felt unduly burdened by NRA codes.
Conscientious about his new duties, Ryan did not miss a
hearing in the board's ten-month life, during which they
heard sixty-nine cases.

Ryan and McGowan were both concerned with the success
of the New Deal. The year 1935 brought the Wagner Act,
which rescued Section 7a from the NRA and set up a National Labor Relations Board to encourage trade union organization, "probably the most just, beneficent, and far-reach-

ing piece of labour legislation ever enacted in the United States," said Ryan. The Social Security Act provided unemployment and old-age insurance. More needed doing, Ryan felt, especially a huge programme of useful public works.

Meanwhile, Fr Coughlin called the President a "liar" and "communistic" and "Franklin Doublecross Roosevelt". He said the choice between the Democrats and Republicans was "between carbolic acid and rat poison". Ryan was angry, but he avoided public comment on Coughlin as long as he could. He did not want to see two Catholic priests engage in a public fight, but as Coughlin usurped the phrase "social justice", was acknowledged to have caused the defeat of U.S. adherence to the World Court, and was generally misleading his millions of listeners on Catholic social thought, Ryan finally agreed when the Democratic National Committee, Senator Joseph O'Mahoney, and James Hoey, then Collector of Internal Revenue in New York, insisted that he reply to Coughlin.

Ryan took up all the major issues, denied that men like Frankfurter and Tugwell, Sidney Hillman and David Dubinsky were Communists, as charged by Coughlin, and declared that anyone who called them that was bound in conscience to restore their good name. Roosevelt's great achievement was in stopping Communism, said Ryan, and if he's defeated, Communism will have an opportunity it is now denied. He called Coughlin's "explanation of our economic maladies at least fifty-nine per cent wrong, and . . . his monetary theories are at least ninety per cent wrong." Coughlin's monetary theories and proposals, Ryan asserted, have no support in the social encyclicals, and "I think I know something about those encyclicals myself". Ryan spoke rapidly in a colorless voice. He finished ahead of his allotted time. It was not a task he liked, but one he felt he had to do.

In 1938, to Fr Ryan's great delight, Roosevelt called for and Congress enacted a public works programme and primed the pump further through building a two-ocean navy. That same year also saw passage of the Fair Labor Standards

Act, which eventually set up a minimum wage of forty cents an hour and a minimum work week of forty hours for certain businesses engaged in interstate commerce. The Act did not go so far in wages, hours, or coverage, as Ryan wished, but its passage presented a triumph. In 1940, partly as the result of work by Ryan and McGowan, the United States bishops issued a statement on "The Church and the Social Order," which warned against industry's abuse of power, stressed the legitimacy of unions and of strikes when necessary as a means of bringing about a greater equality in union-management relations. The bishops called upon business and industry to provide "not merely a living wage for the moment, but also a saving wage for the future against sickness, old age, death, and unemployment".

After the President's death in April, 1945, Ryan wrote an article for the *Review of Politics,* in which he said the National Labor Relations Act, the Fair Labor Standards Act, and the Social Security Act "have done more to promote social justice than all the other federal legislation enacted since the adoption of the Constitution". It was the last article that Monsignor Ryan ever wrote. He was ill, and after months in the hospital, he insisted on returning home. He died on September 16th, 1945.

When Philip Murray became president of the CIO, the Congress of Industrial Organizations, in 1940, World War II was still in progress. Murray proposed the Industry Council Plan, which he said "follows the encyclical (*Quadragesimo Anno*) almost completely." According to this plan, each defence industry would set up a council with authority to introduce more efficient methods of production to encourage union-management cooperation. Decisions would be made by a board on which labour and management would have equal representation and on which there would be one impartial person representing the government. The inevitable tasks of coordination would be handled by a top National Board of Review, on which labour, management and government would be equally represented.

The Industry Council Plan was not adopted, but its idea was carried out in the Human Relations Committee, set up as an instrument of year-round communication between the steel companies and the United Steel Workers, organized and headed by Murray; so far as apprentices are concerned, in the Plumbers and Pipefitters, and on many varied matters, in the Ladies' Garment Workers. Arthur Goldberg, who had been general counsel for the Steelworkers and later became Secretary of Labour, Supreme Court Justice, and Ambassador to the United Nations, and George Meany, when he became president of the American Federation of Labor and Congress of Industrial Organizations, advocated a form of the plan, which finally resulted in the Labor-Management Advisory Committee set up by President Kennedy. Goldberg was chairman of the committee, with the Secretary of Commerce another "public" member. The original committee included Meany, and several other Catholics as labour members, among them Tom Kennedy, president of the United Mine Workers, and Joseph Keenan, secretary of the International Brotherhood of Electrical Workers. Original management and public members were some of the nation's most outstanding persons.

The President's Advisory Committee on Labor-Management Policy, at least in its early years, sought to do no more than to bring labour, management and public leaders together to discuss common problems such as unemployment, automation, apprenticeship programmes, foreign trade, increased productivity, civil rights, and other current issues free from the urgency and heat of the bargaining table and the inhibiting glare of publicity.

While CIO president, Murray had the problem of ousting the Communists from the ranks of CIO unions. John L. Lewis, as first president of the CIO, was more intent on getting the organizing job done than he was vigilant against infiltration. Most of the party members "disguised themselves as liberals or as American radicals in the democratic tradition," as Max Kampelman put it. Many got in because they were zealous, skilled operators. By 1938, Kampelman reports "Communists had positions of trust, responsibility, and authority giving them complete or partial control in at least forty per cent of the CIO unions, including the United Automobile Workers, the Transport Workers, the American Communications Association, the Newspaper Guild, the United Electrical Workers, the United Public Workers, the National Maritime Union, the Office and Professional Workers, the Woodworkers of America, and the Cannery, Agricultural, Packing, and Allied workers." Communist influence even included Lee Pressman, CIO general counsel, and Len De-Caux, editor of the *CIO News*. Pressman was secretary of the key resolutions committee at conventions.

Murray, a devout Catholic and undeviating anti-Communist, feared a split within the CIO, since the party controlled unions with a membership of a million workers. ACTU aided him. In New York, they purged the Transport Workers which although about four-fifths Catholic, had been taken over. ACTU aided James B. Carey in the Electrical Workers, and was a major factor in the defeat of the Communist faction in the Auto Workers election of 1946. The ACTU members organized themselves as thoroughly as the Communists, showed as much zeal, skill and persistence, and were of major importance in the fight within unions. The labour schools, set up all over the country, were another major factor, since they trained Catholic workers not only in the principles of social justice, but also in public speaking, parliamentary law, and Communist tactics.

Murray had to do his own job, of course. By 1946, he had obtained power to institute proceedings through the CIO Executive Board for the removal of council officers and seizure of council property and funds. He revoked the charters of councils when they refused to follow the new rules, set up new councils, and in the conventions and elsewhere fought the Communists whom he called "ideological dive bombers," "degraded thinkers," and "afflictions on mankind". In his Scottish burr, he told the Communists "either get clear in the CIO or get clear out". The fight was finally successful; Communists in the CIO were eventually "clear out". Today only a few unions, all outside the AFL-CIO ranks, are dominated by Communists.

Meany, long before he became president of the AFL, was opposing Communists overseas. The AFL, during World War II, was one of the few American organizations of any kind to warn against Communist Russia, while maintaining the necessity of cooperation until the Nazis were defeated. It was one of the few organizations to call upon the United States to stop the Chinese Communists on the mainland "while there was yet time". In 1945, after the war, Meany, who was the federation spokesman on international affairs, went to the British Trades Union Congress in Blackpool, England, to warn against admittance of the Soviet Union to the World Trade Union Congress.

The BTU, the French CGT, the Dutch, the Belgians, the Italians, even the CIO, did not heed Meany at the time. Later all of the free trade unions left the WTUC, which was by then an obvious Communist tool, and joined the AFL in the International Confederation of Free Trade Unions, which Meany led in establishing. Even within the ICFTU, the fighting plumber had his troubles. At one time it was dominated by European Socialists and at others it spent too much time writing reports and too little doing anything worth reporting, according to Meany. At another time, Meany fought against admission of Yugoslavia's trade unions. He was against admitting any federation from a totalitarian country, whether the Soviet Union, its satellites, Yugoslavia, Spain, or Peron's Argentina.

Meany's first objective when he became president of the AFL in 1952 was to merge with the CIO. This was effected in 1955, with Meany then heading the merged organizations. His next task was the elimination of racketeering in AFL-CIO unions, and the establishment of an Ethical Practices

Committee. His current objective has so far resulted only in the President's Advisory Committee on Labor-Management Policy.

Under Meany, the AFL-CIO has sought government action to reduce unemployment, which remained at unusually high levels into the 1960's; called for free education for all able young people through two years of college; federal aid to education in both public and parochial elementary and high schools; old-age pensions adequate to meet the needs of the elderly, while AFL-CIO unions sought to improve private pension plans through collective bargaining; hospital insurance for the aged; a housing programme that would enable every family to have proper housing at a price or rent they can afford; elimination of tax loopholes that defeat the principle of taxation based on ability to pay, civil rights, and other measures to improve the welfare of the worker and his family. The AFL led the way to the inclusion of the International Bill of Rights in the United Nations charter, at a time when observers thought the movement a failure; to the disclosure, with specific maps, of slave labour camps in the Soviet Union.

Fr McGowan became director of the NCWC Social Action Department after the death of Father Ryan, and when McGowan became ill, he was in turn succeeded by Mgr George G. Higgins. Higgins was appointed to the staff of the Department in 1944, named assistant director in 1946, and became director in November, 1954. No priest personally knows more trade union leaders in the United States and other countries than Mgr Higgins. He sits down to discuss trade union problems on an intimate footing with Socialists, Christian Democrats, Democrats and Republicans.

Fr McGowan, when director of the Social Action Department, told the United Steelworkers convention in 1950:

> The working people have not only the right to organize, they have the duty to organize. The working people have the duty to pay for themselves and their dependants the cost of the food, clothing, fuel, shelter, medical care, schooling

and religious care that they need to live, and to live well, so that they can live humanly, morally and religiously well. The lone working man cannot get all this on his own. The union can. Therefore, every worker has not only the right to organize, but the duty to organize. It is as simple as that.

Father McGowan's statement is one of the many arguments made by Catholic leaders against the "Right-to-Work" laws. John H. Sheehan, associate professor of economics at the University of Notre Dame, pointed out in an article in *Ave Maria,* April 23rd, 1955, that those who argue for Right-to-Work legislation, among whom are a few Catholic priests, say that no man should be obliged to join a union. He compared this to saying that one can be a citizen of "a community, but should have the right not to pay school and playground taxes, because they themselves have grown up and do not need schools and playgrounds any more. The major intent behind so-called Right-to-Work laws seems to be an attempt by law to lessen or stifle union effectiveness, by destroying union security provisions. At least this is the end achieved."

Mgr Higgins in his Labour Day Mass sermon in 1964 said this:

> Too few Americans in all walks of life are willing to go the whole way and to take the unconditional and unqualified position that secure and stable unions are indispensable prerequisites of a sound social order.
>
> Until this principle is more or less universally taken for granted as a self-evident truth, labour and management will spend too much time and energy sparring with one another—time and energy which they ought to devote to carrying out the demands which social justice makes on both of them. Social justice demands among other things, that the two groups forget their petty differences and jointly try to figure out how they can best serve the welfare, not only of their own members and their own stockholders, but of all their fellow citizens.
>
> In the final analysis, then, the spirit of Labour Day is eminently positive and constructive. What labour and management need more than anything else and what they have a right to expect from all of us on Labour Day is encouragement and,

above all, the support of our continued prayers. They know that their past performance leaves something to be desired and, by and large, they are honestly looking for new ways and means of serving the public interest more effectively.

These statements are certainly in the spirit of Ryan and Dietz, who so well plotted the paths of the Church and Labour in the twentieth century in the United States.

THE CHRISTIAN TRADE UNIONS

The International Federation of Christian Trade Unions, according to its declaration of principles, "is based on and inspired by Christian principles and ethics". It came into being, as its Catholic founders saw it, because it was necessary. In 1908, when the forerunner of the IFCTU was set up, the major trade unions in continental Europe were doctrinaire Marxist Socialists, with close political ties with the Socialist parties. It was not until years after Nicolai Lenin declared Moscow to be the international headquarters of world Socialism, otherwise Communism, that Western European Socialists took the pictures of Marx and the Red flags off their walls and became militantly anti-Communist.

The IFCTU was established in 1920 at The Hague, claiming 3,367,000 members, most of them in the Christian trade unions in Germany and Italy, both of which were destroyed when the Fascists took over. After World War II, the IFCTU had to rise again, but its new main bases were France, the Netherlands and Belgium. After the war, some Christian trade unions, such as those in the Basque, in Spain, and *Confederazione Generale del Lavaro* (CISL) in Italy, affiliated with the International Confederation of Free Trade Unions. In Germany, where occupation forces helped reestablish free trade unions, no provisions were made for Christian trade unions. The American Federation of Labor, as represented by a Catholic trade unionist, Joseph Keenan, now secretary of the International Brotherhood of Electrical Workers, concentrated on establishing a unified, anti-Communist trade union movement, in the DGB, *Deutsche Gewerkschafts Bund*. During the war, the AFL had aided German trade union leaders who went underground or found exile in England, and when World War II was over, helped the DGB establish itself again by furnishing office furniture, typewriters and even funds. Today the Confederation of German Christian Trade Unions (the CGB, *Christlicher Gewerkshaftsbund Deutschlands*), claims 200,000 members, but this is declared to be an inflated figure.

The Catholic Workers Organization (*Katholische Arbeiter Bewegung,* KAB), is not a trade union federation, but an organization of Catholics interested in "Catholic social action as defined by the popes from the time of Leo XIII to Paul". KAB was active in the unsuccessful, gravely handicapped effort to establish democracy in Germany in the Weimar Republic, following World War I. It is active today through the Christian Democratic Union and its numerous schools and parish, diocesan and national groups.

SELECT BIBLIOGRAPHY

In this series: CARTHY, Mother Mary Peter: *Catholicism in English-Speaking Lands* (British edn., *Catholicism in English-Speaking Countries*); HOLLIS, Christopher: *Christianity and Economics* (British edn., *The Church and Economics*); WOODRUFF, Douglas: *Church and State* (British edn., *Church and State in History*); ZAHN, Gordon: *What is Society?*

ABELL, Aaron I.: *American Catholicism and Social Action,* South Bend, Indiana, Notre Dame University, 1963.

BROWNE, Henry J.: *The Catholic Church and the Knights of Labor,* Washington, D.C., Catholic University of America Press, 1949.

CLARK, Colin: *The Conditions of Economic Progress,* New York, St Martin's Press and London, Macmillan, 1957.

COLE, G. D. H.: *A Short History of the British Working Class Movement, 1789-1925,* London, George Allen and Unwin, Ltd., 1926.

CRONIN, John F.: *Social Principles for Economic Life,* Milwaukee, Bruce, 1964.

————: *Christianity and Social Progress,* Baltimore, Helicon, 1965.

FREMANTLE, Anne (Editor): *The Papal Encyclicals in their Historical Context,* New York, New American Library of World Literature, 1956.

HALES, E. E. Y.: *The Catholic Church in the Modern World,* London, Eyre and Spottiswoode, 1958.

KAMPELMAN, Max M.: *The Communist Party vs. the CIO,* New York, Praeger, 1957.

MOODY, Joseph N. (Editor): *Church and Society,* New York, Arts, 1953.

PETRIE, John: *The Worker Priests,* New York and London, Macmillan, 1956.

WARD, Maisie: *France Pagan?,* New York, Sheed and Ward, 1964.